THE
TRIUMPH
OF FAITH

THE TRIUMPH OF FAITH

STRENGTHENING YOUR FAITH AND FAMILY IN TURBULENT TIMES

MELAGITONE SIMANU

Torn Curtain Publishing
Wellington, New Zealand
www.torncurtainpublishing.com

© Copyright 2021 Melagitone Simanu. All rights reserved.

ISBN Softcover 978-0-6489823-7-1

No portion of this book may be reproduced, stored in a retrieval system or transmitted in any form or by any means—electronic, mechanical, photocopy, recording or otherwise—except for brief quotations in printed reviews of promotion, without prior written permission from the author.

All text in bold or in parentheses are the author's own.

Unless otherwise noted, all scripture is taken from the New King James Version. Copyright © 1982 by Thomas Nelson, Inc. Used by permission. All rights reserved.

Scripture quotations marked NIV are taken from the New International Version®, NIV®. Copyright © 1973, 1978, 1984, 2011 by Biblica, Inc.™ Used by permission of Zondervan. All rights reserved worldwide.

Scripture quotations marked (NLT) are taken from the Holy Bible, New Living Translation, copyright ©1996, 2004, 2015 by Tyndale House Foundation. Used by permission of Tyndale House Publishers, Carol Stream, Illinois 60188. All rights reserved.

Scripture quotations marked (NASB) are taken from the New American Standard Bible®, Copyright © 1960, 1971, 1977, 1995, 2020 by The Lockman Foundation. Used by permission. All rights reserved. www.lockman.org.

Scriptures marked (KJV) are taken from the King James Version of the Bible.

Cataloguing in Publishing Data
Title: The Triumph of Faith
Author: Melagitone Simanu
Subjects: Christian Faith, Biblical teaching, Christian life.

A copy of this title is held at the National Library of Australia.

Your word is a lamp to my feet and a light to my path.

Psalm 119:105

DEDICATION

This book is devoted and dedicated to my Lord, Savior and King—Jesus Christ, who has gifted me with salvation and drawn me into His abundant life. Most of all, He has provided divine courage and revelation, so that I am enabled to preach His Word of truth. What a privilege! Without You in my life, Jesus, I am nothing!

My Beloved Wife & Daughters

To my loving and fearless wife and my beautiful daughters—you are my prayer warriors, my powerful intercessors, and the ones who fill me with divine motivation. It is your sacrificial support and love that have encouraged me to pursue and fulfil the calling of God in my life. You are all a blessing and a gift from God for me, and I cherish the responsibility to care for you. I love and appreciate you all so much. A family who serves and honors God together in unity and love is indestructible, and that is what we have together. Thank You, Jesus!

My Dearest Loving Parents

To my late father, Faleao Ieru Sapolu—you were a mighty and faithful man of God, and the blessing you carried endures even though you are now with our Lord Jesus.

And to my courageous and godly mother, Situpu Sapolu. Even now, you continue to serve God wholeheartedly and with full devotion. Together, you have blessed me with the gift of life and were also the first to plant the seed of God's Word in me. You led me to Jesus Christ, to receive salvation as a young adult, and I know you never cease to pray for me, my family, and especially the ministry God has entrusted to me. Thank you so much, Mum and Dad. I love you both and always will.

Glory to Jesus!

CONTENTS

Foreword		11
Introduction		13
Chapter One	Overcome the Spirit of Fear	17
Chapter Two	Called to Be a Watchman	29
Chapter Three	Rekindle the Lamp in Your Home	49
Chapter Four	Led by the Spirit	61
Chapter Five	Hold onto the Vision	73
Chapter Six	Faithfully Run Your Race	87
Chapter Seven	Destroying Giants	99
Prayer of Salvation		125
Author's Note		127
Acknowledgements		129
About the Author		131

FOREWORD

We are living in challenging and unprecedented times. We only have to turn on the news to see that people all around the globe are facing uncertainty, stress, and fear as the effects of virulent disease, economic upheaval, national unrest and racism, climate change concerns, natural disasters, to name a few, are on the rise.

Current events have caused us to consider how things seem to be gradually moving towards centralized control, as predicted in end-times Bible prophecies. But in the midst of this turbulence, we have the Word of God. Our God reigns and we take comfort in the eternal truth, that He is in control. The integrity of His Word gives us stability and confidence. Jesus promises us His peace, and cautions that our hearts are not to be troubled or afraid. True peace and hope are ours when we invite Jesus into our heart.

Pastor Melagitone Simanu has a heart for people being grounded in the Word. He addresses fear as a spirit that brings torment from the enemy and teaches us how to overcome it and embrace an opposite spirit, which comes from God—a spirit of power, love and a sound mind. The message he brings will instill courage and resilient faith, inspiring the reader to fulfil their life's purpose and destiny in God. Most importantly, Pastor Melagitone writes about how the mighty Holy Spirit has been assigned as our Helper, the One who will lead and guide us through the affairs of life, if we allow Him.

I have known Pastor Melagitone Simanu for nearly twenty years, and we have developed a close, personal relationship. For twelve years he served as an Elder and Associate Pastor for our church in Auckland before moving to Australia so he and his wife, Mareta, could take up leadership roles in pastoral care, teaching of the Word, and praise and worship ministry. This aligns with their passion that our worship be in spirit and in truth, and that purity in our daily lives should reflect that priority.

They are presently the Senior Pastors for Divine Revelation Worship Centre in Melton, Victoria, where they are doing a great work to the glory of God. It is a privilege to write the foreword for this book, in what may very well be the first of many.

Leuli Ieriko
Senior Pastor
Mangere Worship Centre Christian Church
Auckland, New Zealand

INTRODUCTION

I have been a believer in Jesus Christ for more than twenty years and along the way, the Word of God—the Bible—has been my source of truth. Those truths have been life-giving to me. For many years now, as a preacher and teacher delivering God's Word to His people, I have found that it is insufficient to merely 'talk the talk.' Rather, it is vital to embody what we say and *live it out* in our day to day lives.

The Lord has revealed so much of His Word to me over the course of these years, speaking to my spirit every day. In fact, this has developed in me a desire—one could even say a 'call'—to share these revelations with you in these pages.

We must seriously take to heart God's design for us to be doers of His Word, appreciating and applying God's laws and His guiding principles that we find laid out for us there. People are never transformed through empty words, but when we invite the Word of God to speak into our midst, hearts are moved. As His Word pierces into every internal part of their being, we witness miraculous transformation in people's life. The Bible declares,

> *All scripture is given by inspiration of God, and is profitable for doctrine, for reproof, for correction, for instruction in righteousness, that the man of God may be thoroughly equipped for every good work.*
>
> **2 Timothy 3:16-17**

I believe that every person God created has an opportunity to be encouraged and transformed if they honestly and wholeheartedly open themselves to God's infallible Word of truth and life!

The Lord has planted a desire in my heart to write this book. It comes from a collection of my own preaching notes, taken from both sermons and training sessions I have led. My prayer and desire for every reader is that these words of encouragement will bless your heart and strengthen your faith as you pursue the will of God, drawing forth spiritual healing and deliverance in your life, and sparking into flame a life of victory in Jesus Christ, our Lord, Savior, and King.

As a believer and servant of our Lord Jesus Christ my constant prayer is that you would live with honor, fully activated into your calling, and above all else that you would experience a victorious lifestyle in line with God's Word.

It is my hope and expectation that the Spirit of God will bring fresh revelation through these pages to refresh and encourage you, and to minister to you spiritually, emotionally, physically and mentally as you continue running your race for Jesus!

> *For the word of God is living and powerful, and sharper than any two-edged sword, piercing even to the division of soul and spirit, and of joints and marrow, and is a discerner of the thoughts and intents of the heart. And there is no creature hidden from His sight, but all things*

are naked and open to the eyes of Him to whom we must give account.

Hebrews 4:12-13

My love to you all in Jesus' Name. Glory and honor to Him alone!

- Chapter One -

OVERCOME THE SPIRIT OF FEAR

If we are to understand and lay hold of a life that is free from fear and full of faith, we need to have a clear understanding of those two words—*fear* and *faith*.

Fear is mentioned in the Bible many times, and it presents in two ways. Sometimes it carries a positive connotation, describing a posture in which we honor or reverence God. At other times, fear refers to something *undesirable*, an unpleasant emotion of anxiety or apprehension in the face of threat or danger or pain.

Faith stands in contrast to fear. It is a theme that runs throughout the Bible, from the beginning of Genesis to the end of the New Testament. In Hebrews 11:1 (NIV) we are told that faith is confidence in what we hope for, and "assurance about what we do not see." Faith describes complete trust in someone or something; it is the strong foundation on which we build our lives.

In our world, fear and anxiety are rampant. The fear that arises in our hearts and minds can be due to human or physical threats, but can also be the result of an evil, spiritual attack of Satan. In fact, fear is often caused by spiritual affliction. Faith also functions in the spiritual realm. This is why we must deal with fear in the secret place of the Most High God, placing our trust and confidence in God and in the promises of His Word.

In reality, these words, *faith* and *fear* are opposites; in the spiritual realm, they work against one another, they are at enmity with each other! When fear has the louder voice within us, our faith in God diminishes. But when the voice of *faith* is stronger, fear is weakened and eventually loses its hold in our lives. Let's be people who place our faith in God and His Word, standing against the fear that Satan and his demonic forces endeavor to bring into our lives through the threat of harm or hardship.

We are in a season where people around the world have trembled with fear because of an unseen and unpredictable threat—a global pandemic. Many have been living with anxiety, unable to escape the onslaught of the Coronavirus. Meanwhile, scientists and medical experts have labored hard, pooling their collective experience and knowledge to find a cure. We, as God's people, have a choice—will we give way to *fear*, or be strong in *faith*? Seeking Him within the Word determines which of these two we will manifest in our lives as the children of God. It is the Word of God that will empower and encourage us as we go through such circumstances. Let us thank our Heavenly Father, knowing we serve a mighty God who guards us and shelters us under His divine protection. *Hallelujah!*

When the Moabites, Ammonites and Meunites declared war on Jehoshaphat and word arrived that a vast army was coming against him from Edom (on the other side of the sea), fear entered King Jehoshaphat. He was alarmed and afraid. Why? Because when he looked through his natural eyes, the first thing he saw was the physical reality—a multitude of people coming to attack him. Jehoshaphat needed to view the situation from heaven's perspective!

In 2 Chronicles 20:14 we read that the Spirit of the Lord came on Jahziel, the son of Zechariah, who spoke to the people and said,

> *Listen, all you of Judah and you inhabitants of Jerusalem, and you, King Jehoshaphat! Thus says the Lord to you: Do not be afraid nor dismayed because of this great multitude, for the battle is not yours, but God's. Tomorrow go down against them. They will surely come up by the Ascent of Ziz, and you will find them at the end of the brook before the Wilderness of Jeruel. You will not need to fight in this battle. Position yourselves, stand still and see the salvation of the Lord, who is with you, O Judah and Jerusalem! Do not fear or be dismayed;*

tomorrow go out against them, for the Lord is with you.

2 Chronicles 20:15-17

The key verse here is verse 17: "Do not be afraid nor dismayed . . . for the battle is not yours, but God's." This was how God saw the situation, and Jehoshaphat needed to view the battle the same way. He needed a new perspective on what was happening.

In our journey as born-again Christians, we continue to grow in faith from one stage to the next—even so, we can tend to easily lose hope the moment fear seeks to enter our lives. Over the past few years, many of us have experienced peace. Everything we touched worked just as we expected. We enjoyed the normality of going to shopping malls, driving around freely, dining in our favorite restaurants, enjoying opportunities to gather, and visiting our best-loved places. When the Covid-19 pandemic entered the scene, however, we faced what many describe as a 'new normal,' one in which fear became prevalent in many lives.

We live in a season where reports continually announce the undesirable effects of this virus, overwhelmingly sowing uncertainty and fear. The tendency is to respond by cowering within the comfort of our houses, fearful of catching the disease from others, even immediate families and friends.

How can we get rid of the anxieties and frightening emotions that hinder our faith from resting on the promises of God in our lives? Perhaps the solution to overcoming the fear we face can be found in the story of Jehoshaphat. His story, along with many others in the Bible, show us powerful ways to overcome the spirit of fear.

Take Refuge in the Secret Place

2 Chronicles 20:1-5 tells us that when Jehoshaphat heard about the army and the multitude coming to attack him, he was alarmed, but he resolved immediately to inquire of the Lord for an answer, and proclaimed a fast for all Judah. The people of Judah came together to seek help from the Lord through prayers and fasting. *Glory to God!*

We should follow Jehoshaphat's example when trials and challenges hit us. As God's children, we should rise up, seeking *Him* for a solution and trusting Him with all our hearts. Let's endeavor to cast out all fear, and live our lives accordingly to the words of our Lord Jesus Christ. The moment we cry out to God, He will hear us if we seek and pray to Him by faith. *Faith*, not fear, is what makes us overcomers! *Hallelujah!*

David also faced great fear, but found refuge in the secret place of the Most High God. He reminds us of the safety and protection of those who dwell in the presence of the Lord, that God is our refuge and our fortress, in whom we trust. Psalm 91:3-6 says,

> *Surely, He shall deliver you from the snare of the fowler and from the perilous pestilence. He shall cover you with His feathers, and under His wings you shall take refuge; His truth shall be your shield and buckler. You shall not*

> be afraid of the terror by night, nor of the arrow that flies by day, nor of the pestilence that walks in the darkness, nor of the plague that destroys at noonday.

When we truly understand the Word of God, and realize, as David did, that we can take refuge in the secret place of the Most High God, *nothing* will make us worry or cause us to live in fear. Psalm 91 assures us that even *diseases, pestilence and plagues* will have no effect against us, because we are kept safe; sheltered in the secret dwelling place of God Almighty we are saturated with His presence and covered by the precious blood of Jesus.

ACTIVATE THE WORD OF GOD

As we meditate on the words of Jesus and come into agreement with Him, we drive away the spirit of fear and are able to dwell in His love and enjoy His peace. In 2 Timothy 1:7 we are reminded that, "God has not given us a spirit of fear, but of power and of love and of a sound mind." *Amen!*

The Word of God is concise and clear; we need to activate His words and let them abide in our hearts. If the Lord has truly given us a spirit of power and a sound mind, let's strengthen our faith in Him and trust Him wholeheartedly. If your circumstances and all that is going on in the world are causing you to live in fear, I urge you today to take time to reflect. What is the source of your fear? I confess that there are times I have felt worried and afraid, simply because it is in our human nature to feel all these emotions.

You and I, however, as believers who have been equipped and taught in the Word and ways of the Lord, have the opportunity to understand the heart of the Heavenly Father towards His children even in difficult circumstances. Today, evaluate your faith in God. Embrace His words of truth and life and learn to speak them confidently over your situation!

OVERCOME FEAR BY FAITH

Hebrews 11:6 tells us that without faith it is impossible to please God. In other words, God is looking for faith so that He can answer our prayers! The Bible tells us that even the smallest expression of faith is enough to move mountains (Matthew 17:20). Let's pray, knowing that all those who call upon Jesus' name *in faith* will be heard and answered. We need to replace our fear-filled prayers with prayers of faith!

As a part of the precious family of God, be encouraged. The Word of God always exhorts us to be strong and courageous during trials and sufferings in our lives. We only overcome the spirit of fear and live a peaceful life as we activate our faith and trust God wholeheartedly.

In Deuteronomy 31:6 Moses exhorted God's people with the words, "Be strong and of good courage, do not fear or be afraid . . . for the Lord your God, He is the One who goes with you. He will not leave you nor forsake you." The Lord abides with those who keep and activate His words, who live by faith and not by sight. No matter what Satan and his evil forces (or the circumstances of life) throw at you to drag you down, move and pray in the power of the Holy Spirit, and keep serving God with a true heart of faith.

We know that God could simply reach out and save us from global pandemics or any of life's other challenges, but instead, He uses these times to test our faith and cause us to grow. The Scriptures tell us that in the last days we can expect to see different trials and troubling situations in the world—these are some of the signs that indicate that the coming of Jesus Christ is near.

Until then, He has given us His Holy Spirit to empower and strengthen us, to enliven our faith through the anointing and power of the Holy Spirit. When we understand the essential core of our relationship with the Holy Spirit and His ministry in our lives, we can cry out to our Heavenly Father at any time, knowing He will move in power to fulfil every need for us.

THE BATTLE BELONGS TO GOD

God wanted Jehoshaphat to know, "The battle is Mine, not yours." We don't need to fight our battles alone, but rather activate and choose to live in obedience to His Word when He says,

> *You will not need to fight in this battle. Position yourselves, stand still and see the salvation of the Lord, who is with you.*
>
> *2 Chronicles 20:17*

I love how God encourages us to rise up, position ourselves and stand still. Sometimes, the best solution to a problem is to be silent and meditate in God's presence. There is peace to be found when we stand still in His presence and see the salvation of our Lord Jesus with the eyes of faith. There we find ourselves immoveable and unshakeable, standing on His Word until our faith becomes sight!

When God calls us to position ourselves in the realm of the Spirit, to be still and quiet before Him, we *must* obey! Often, we are too busy, lost in our own world, focused only on what is physical. When we become 'busy bodies' here, rather than positioning ourselves in the presence, love, and peace of God, the devil can—and will—toss us anything that could discourage our faith and hem us in until we are left like the world around us, cowering in fear. Let us therefore be aware and on guard at all times. As we stand firm in His promises and in His presence, we will be strengthened to trust Him and obey, and the Holy Spirit will reveal to us what is needed.

Remember, whatever problems and trials we hear and see, both in our lives and in the world around us, God specifically says that the physical battle is not ours to fight. The battle is *spiritual*, and it belongs to the *Lord*. As we engage in spiritual warfare, rising up in faith against the enemy and his demonic forces, let's keep our eyes on Jesus and His victory for us!

It is a simple thing that God is saying: *You need to do nothing other than keep still in His presence and have faith in Him.* Jesus has done everything for us on the cross. He gave us *full* authority and power to destroy the works of the enemy. Consequently, when there is any attempt to threaten us or our spirit, we must activate that power and authority by faith to silence Satan and destroy the spirit of fear in the name of Jesus. *Blessed be the name of the Lord!*

When we stand still on the Word of God, we will see the glory of Jesus upon us; fear will not get a foothold! Let's live and move by faith, with the confidence that we are protected and secured under the wings of our God. Stay assured that the battle belongs to God, that victory is ours through Jesus, our Mighty Lord and Savior. I promise you, when you activate your faith, and trust the Word of Jesus, neither demons, diseases, nor death can threaten you, for you know your true identity in Christ Jesus. Psalm 23:4 says, "Though I walk through the valley of the shadow of death, I will fear no evil."

When we spend our lives trusting and leaning on God's Word with full confidence and faith, the presence of God rests upon us; we receive the *Shekinah* glory, the glory of God that will seal and protect us. With His glory upon us, no disease, nor death, neither any evil forces can come against us; trouble trembles and flees when the glory of God is in our midst. In Isaiah 41:10 we read,

> *Fear not, for I am with you; Be not dismayed, for I am your God. I will strengthen you, Yes, I will help you. I will uphold you with My righteous right hand.*

God has already spoken that we should not fear. Remember, we must overcome the spirit of fear within us.

Have faith in God. Let your heart be still in His presence. Remain firm in His Word, and stand on His divine promises. God is not a man that He should lie, nor a son of man that He should change His mind (Numbers 23:19). We must commit all our ways and cast all our cares upon Jesus, who knows what we need and what is best for our lives. He is the Alpha and Omega, the beginning and the finisher of our faith. God Almighty upholds us with His righteous hand, therefore, we shall not fear! *Glory and honor to Jesus!*

Thank you, Father God, for Your Word of truth. In Jesus' name I cast out any spirit of fear in me right now. I am more than a conqueror; Jesus has already won the battle for me on the cross. I claim and decree the spirit of love and a sound mind upon my life, so that I may continue to enjoy Your salvation and peace. I thank You, Jesus, for I no longer live in fear but in faith and confidence in Your divine peace. In Your mighty name, Lord Jesus, I pray. Praise be to God forever and ever. Amen and Amen!

- Chapter Two -

CALLED TO BE A WATCHMAN

As the family of Jesus Christ, we live in difficult times. Many people, in the face of severe testing, have walked away from their faith in Christ, while others have overcome and drawn nearer to Him despite the personal struggles they face. What makes the difference?

We know from Scripture that we are living in the 'last days,' and that if we are to keep our faith strong throughout trials, we must lean on God's promise that He will never leave us, nor forsake us! Let's allow the Word of God to be our source of strength and keep us firm in the peace Jesus gives. We must, however, rise up during these times. Not only are we called to rely on the Word of God—we must also proclaim it! Like Ezekiel, you are *called to be a watchman!*

> *Again, the word of the Lord came to me, saying, 'Son of man, speak to the children of your people, and say to them: "When I bring the sword upon a land, and the people of the land take a man from their territory and make him their watchman, when he sees the sword coming upon the land, if he blows the trumpet and warns the people, then whoever hears the sound of the trumpet and does not take warning, if the sword comes and takes him away, his blood shall be on his own head. He heard the sound of the trumpet, but did not take warning; his blood shall be upon himself. But he who takes warning will save his life. But if the watchman sees the sword coming and does not blow the trumpet, and the people are not warned, and the sword comes and takes any person from among them, he is taken away in his iniquity; but his blood I will require at the watchman's hand." So you, son of man: I have made you a watchman for the house of Israel; therefore, you shall hear a word from My mouth and warn them for Me.'*
>
> **Ezekiel 33:1-7**

The watch-person had an important role and responsibility to look after, or guard, a building (usually through the night, when an attack was more likely), and to remain on the lookout for danger or trouble.

This is your role, and mine as well. As spiritual leaders in our homes, our job is to keep watch over our families, and as leaders in the House of God, to carefully guard the church that is entrusted to our care. This is a vital position—one which we must take seriously. Scripture makes it clear that if we stand idly by and do nothing in the face of the enemy's threats, the result will be chaos as God's people are hurt and lives destroyed. On the other hand. when we remain spiritually alert, reliable, and responsible, the people entrusted to our care can flourish!

Protect Your Realm

In the Old Testament, watchtowers were strategically located to facilitate two main outcomes. In peacetime, they provided a place to oversee fields so as to protect a nation's supply of crops, farming, and food against surprise attacks. During times of battle, the watchtower was a location from which the access points to a city could be monitored and guarded and the situation constantly assessed.

A watchman's job was to scan the city walls and entrances. If a threat appeared, he would sound a warning and the nation or city would shut its gates and prepare to resist the onslaught of the enemy.

This was Ezekiel's role in the nation of Israel. God appointed him to warn Israel of its sins, and He also told him about the consequences of failing at this task. As a prophet who represented God, it was crucial that he be on guard and stay obedient, faithfully warning the people and deterring them from committing sin.

God is holy, and while His love for the humans He has created is unconditional, He hates sin and its consequences. As Christians who believe in Jesus and understand God's laws and principles, our role as watchmen encompasses our nation, church and family, and it is vital in God's eyes. It is our duty to deliver warnings and to offer instruction when those in our nation, our congregations, or our households, are straying into a life of sin. This is because sin gives the devil a foothold! It creates a breach for the enemy to carry out his destructive purposes in the lives of those we love, and can threaten others under our care. For this reason, we are to sound the Word of God, calling out better choices as we correct and instruct our loved ones to turn from any wicked ways and serve God with reverence, obedience, and love.

OUR SPIRITUAL SENSES

A watch-person who is representing Jesus should have a good spiritual vision—we ought to be able to discern the 'unseen' landscape, scanning for every movement of the enemy. Our spiritual hearing must be finely-tuned as well, our ears open to the voice of the Holy Spirit in order to discern the enemy's lies.

Any person with bad vision or poor eyesight needs a good pair of glasses in order to function well. If our spiritual vision is unclear, we need to look through a spiritual lens so that we do not end up stumbling and frustrated, unable to locate or discern our final destination. We *must not* walk like one who is lost! We must see with the eyes of the Spirit, bringing clarity to those around us.

Similarly, when our ears are not attentive to the voice of God, we can easily miss the gentle promptings of the Holy Spirit who wants to help us. Let's not be deaf to what He says, simply hearing with one ear while it goes out the other! Instead, let us pay attention to what is true, so that we may bring a spirit of hope even to a gloomy situation. Let's position ourselves in the Spirit, keeping our spiritual eyes alert, our ears attentive, and our hearts boldly ready to respond in obedience to His directives.

An Elevated Position

As a watchperson, you must take up your position! A watchman was usually situated on a rooftop, a tower, or a tall building. From this high vantage point he would gain the ability to see for a great distance in all directions and detect any unusual movement.

As watch-people who care for others on behalf of God, we too must operate from an elevated position. We *must* have ears to hear and eyes to see when the devil is about to attack us or those under our care. We too, need a higher perspective. We are seated with Christ in heavenly places, high above all principalities and powers. From there, we are able to see with clarity in the spiritual realm. Let's 'come up higher' in the Spirit, seeking the Lord for divine revelation and spiritual knowledge so we can guard and protect our families.

God's Word says,

> *Where there is no vision, the people perish. But he that keepeth the law, happy is he.*
>
> *Proverbs 29:18 (KJV)*

Without revelation and wisdom from God, communities and nations suffer. We must therefore, make our decisions based on divine revelation, knowing that every decision we make affects the people around us. When we first receive godly wisdom and knowledge, we can be truly effective in our calling as watch-people.

As we serve God faithfully and live a life of obedience to His commands, we become more aware of God's desire to guard and prosper those we love. This is why we all must play our part as leaders in our families, church and society, directing and guiding others in the will and ways of the Lord. Quite simply, let's be watchmen who are alert, spiritually perceptive, sounding the alarm when the enemy attacks, and calling God's people to battle.

AN UNWELCOME CALL

Sometimes the warning a watchman sounds is not welcomed by the people. Some would rather ignore a threat than take it seriously, while others may get upset by the unnecessary disruption it brings. But as spiritual guardians, we cannot afford to sugar-coat what He wants to say simply because we are afraid of being rejected, ignored, or getting hurt. God always stands by His Word, He highly values our role as watch-people in our families and churches, and He will reward us as we guard the peace and safety of those He entrusts to our care.

We must never forget that every battle is ultimately a spiritual battle. Viruses, social problems, economic downturns . . . these may appear to be simply physical issues, but if we address them merely from a physical perspective, we will lose the real battle. The Scriptures tell us that,

> . . . *we do not wrestle against flesh and blood, but against principalities, against powers, against the rulers of the darkness of this age, against spiritual hosts of wickedness in the heavenly places.*
>
> *Ephesians 6:12*

The real battle is always spiritual! Therefore, let us be prepared to engage in spiritual warfare to keep our families protected and safe. Let us gather our families and train them in the Word of God. We must make a bold stand to bring our families into the throne room of God through prayer, fasting, praise and worship, strengthening them through the Word of truth.

Do not let your loved ones wander helplessly like those who have no living hope! It is important that people's inner being—their spirits—are encouraged and fully equipped through the Word of Life.

Be Alert and Prayerful

Jesus told His disciples that He was going to pray to His Father, and asked them to also pray as they waited for Him. Unfortunately, when Jesus came back, they were all asleep!

> *When He rose up from prayer, and had come to His disciples He found them sleeping from sorrow. Then He said to them, "Why do you sleep? Rise and pray, lest you enter into temptation."*
>
> Luke 22:45-46

Are we doing the same thing today? Are we growing tired or weary in our current situation? Whether in times of comfort or restriction, let us not miss the call of the Holy Spirit to persist in prayer, seeking God with all our strength.

As children of God, we must be remain spiritually vigilant, discerning and prayerful at all times. Imagine if the disciples had been diligent in prayer, keeping their eyes and minds wide open while they waited for the Master! What a great lesson to us, the precious family of Christ, to stay alert and be prayerful at all times.

The Bible speaks of "continuing steadfast in prayer" (Romans 12:12). Paul wrote that we should "continue earnestly in prayer, being vigilant in it with thanksgiving" (Colossians 4:2). Likewise, in Ephesians 6:18 we read that we should be, "praying always with all prayer and supplication in the Spirit, being watchful to this end with all perseverance and supplication for all the saints."

One day Jesus will return just as He promised, but in the meantime, He has asked us to stay in prayer! As we wait and partner with Him in prayer, we will bring security and freedom to our families and communities, and will remain undefeated in the face of the enemy.

INCREASING IN THE SPIRIT

As we activate God's Word in our lives, we become more alert and prayerful. Our spiritual weakness is transformed into strength as we allow His Spirit to pour life into us. We are enriched and become wise in all our ways, aware of God's will and aligned with His purposes in our spiritual journey. This is how we, in turn, become a blessing to others! Though the world is in a time of restriction, let us not merely sit at home doing nothing. Instead, let's encourage and strengthen our children so they can be comforted and set free from fear. This is a time to increase our devotion to the Word of God. Wholeheartedly pray and fast, and find victory on your knees as you bring down every threat in the name of Jesus!

Our hearing and alertness in the Spirit must be outstanding if we are to play our part well. As He instructed, we must serve and love the Lord with all our heart, mind and soul. It is essential that we receive the Word of truth deep into our spirits, believing, as Jesus has said, that victory belongs to us, that we are more than overcomers, and that He has won the battle for us through His death on the cross and His glorious resurrection.

Rise up, dear friends, and stay alert in the Spirit! I encourage you again to not waste time, but to speak words of life over your surroundings which will protect and secure your family, church and nation from the enemy's evil attacks. Rise up like warrior princes and princesses in the army of King Jesus. As you dedicate time in the presence of the Holy Spirit, you will be filled with revelation; you will know what to be attentive to and what you must do, and you will receive a sense of divine timing for all the Lord calls you to do.

When we, as watch-people in our family, stay alert and prayerful, activating the Word of God in our lives, nothing can truly distress us. In my experience our families, our children, and those around us will live in peace and harmony, their faith staying strong in God because we have simply done our part in this role.

Think of it like this: In most countries, a security or law-enforcement department is tasked with watching over and protecting the wellbeing and affairs of their citizens. Another department is responsible for weather forecasting, alerting the people when storms and natural disasters threaten a region. These 'watchmen' present warnings so that people can prepare for what is to come and find a place of refuge.

It is the same for us in the Spirit. When Satan comes to attack our families and the body of Christ, we must raise our standard of faith.

> *When the enemy comes in like a flood, The Spirit of the LORD will lift up a standard against him.*
>
> *Isaiah 59:19b*

We must not sit still when we see Satan coming to destroy our family or the body of Christ. We must rise up in victory, wielding the sword of the Spirit and releasing the Word of Jesus from our mouth, pushing back the destructive works of the enemy. When we possess the lifestyle of a pray-er, no evil can truly take root, because the Spirit of God will always establish our faith into new levels of confidence and boldness in the face of the enemy.

As we refuse to allow the enemy a foothold in our territory, let's be encouraged with the words of Scripture:

> *But you belong to God, my dear children. You have already won a victory over those people, because the Spirit who lives in you is greater than the spirit who lives in the world.*
>
> *1 John 4:4 (NLT)*

Fix Your Focus

When we lift our level of faith, we position ourselves to grow in discernment and sensitivity to the Spirit. Maturing in these ways is like adjusting the focus on your camera when you take a picture. You need to adjust the settings to ensure a good quality image. When we adjust our focus and see through a lens of faith, we get a clearer picture of what

God sees. Likewise, we must adjust our stance in the Spirit if we are to get a better perspective on what God intends for our situation.

Initially, our focus may be fixed on discerning Satan's attacks, but when we change our focus to the leading of the Holy Spirit, everything shifts! I declare over you today that it doesn't matter which angle the devil is shooting from— your focus is right on target! You are a wise and an alert watch-person! *Hallelujah!*

No matter how many times Satan and his evil forces try to attack our families and churches, he will never get through us because the glory of God's Spirit is upon us, and our eyes are fixed on Him! With the living Word of God as our source, and the Holy Spirit as our Helper powerfully activating the Word of God in us, we will prevail.

KNOW HIS VOICE

There is a promise of blessing as we stay true to our calling as watch-men and women, but here is the key: You must be familiar with the voice of God's Spirit. The book of Deuteronomy gives us assurance of blessings if we diligently obey the voice of the Lord.

> *Now it shall come to pass, if you diligently obey the voice of the Lord your God, to observe carefully all His commandments which I command you today, that the Lord your God will set you high above all nations of the earth. And all these blessings shall come upon you*

and overtake you, because you obey the voice of the Lord your God.

Deuteronomy 28:1-2

The emphasis in this passage is on the exhortation to *'hear'* and *'obey.'* Hearing and obedience require an attentiveness to God's voice and a humble heart that is willing to submit to what He says. Regardless of the amount of times God speaks to us through His Holy Spirit, if our ears are not hearing properly, or if our hearts are stubborn and disobedient, we risk missing out on receiving His blessings. Instead, let us determine to tune our ears to His voice, respond in obedience, and help our loved ones rise up in love for Him!

LIVE HOLY LIVES

The story of Eli and his sons serves as a wakeup call in our generation. Eli was a man whom God called and chose to be a priest, *a watchman* in the house of the Lord. Eli had a high calling; a blessing was upon his generational lineage, and yet his ending was not good. Eli saw his sons doing wrong in the eyes of God, but he did nothing to bring them the discipline they required. Not only that, his sons committed adultery and openly indulged in their unholy desires, even while serving in the temple!

What a lesson to us. We must not turn a blind eye, pretending everything around us is fine, when in fact, our children may be falling apart or living a displeasing life in rebellion towards God. Let's not remain silent when we see our children being lured into the cursed traps of the enemy, doing nothing to correct, encourage and strengthen them so they can turn back to God and His ways.

The truth is, the God that we serve is holy, and if we are to live in a way that is pleasing in His sight, we who serve and worship Him must live holy lives. As watch-people, we have an assignment, a call of God on our lives. Our mandate is to love the Lord our God with all our heart and to fulfil the commission Jesus left us. However, we also have a responsibility to lead our families well.

What happened to Eli and his family is indeed sad, but the effect of their sin didn't stop there—his family line was unable to continue to function in the priesthood. Praise God that today, our sins are covered by the blood of Jesus! Our task as parents, is to be diligent to apply the blood over our families and homes, the blood that cancels sin and drives out fear. Let's ensure our children are covered, so they may rise into the calling on their lives with confidence and joy.

With love, I speak from the bottom of my heart, releasing what God has revealed to me to strengthen you all. I speak directly to you as fathers or mothers—don't ever leave your children to wander, exposed to Satan's evil schemes. Do not allow your sons or daughters to do whatever their flesh desires. Rather, draw them into the Word. God's Word is alive and will complete its work in their lives. If you as parents continue to set an example by heeding the Holy Spirit's voice, walking in obedience, and staying alert, your children will take notice and will be ready to receive their godly heritage. I assure you, the favor and goodness of God will follow you and your children, from one generation to the next. *Praise God!*

You, however, must take your job seriously to train and equip your children in the ways of the Lord. The responsibility to nurture and strengthen your children rests with you. No matter how old they are, if you know that your son or daughter is drifting into sin or wandering from the faith, you must be strong and courageous to intervene, tirelessly contending for them in prayer and speaking the truth they need to hear. You must rise up as a parent who loves your child, serving as their watchman, giving them sound warnings, and preparing them for spiritual warfare and victory on the battlefield against the enemy.

If we as parents do not carry out our task well, or fail to warn and discipline our children, the results are nearly unthinkable. To continue to walk in disobedience and rebellion against the ways of God is a sure path to spiritual and physical ruin. No parent wishes the blood of their dear children to be upon their head. Let us resolve to fulfil our God-given roles and responsibilities. In so doing, we will avoid the grief, disgrace and heaviness of heart that comes from a ruined life, and instead, safeguard joy for the next generation.

The Proverbs are filled with amazing wisdom that can help us to teach our children in the ways of the Lord. In Proverbs 22:6 we read, "Train up a child in a way he should go, and when he is old he will not depart from it."

Likewise, Proverbs 23:13 (NIV) says,

> *Do not withhold discipline from a child; if you punish them with the rod, they will not die. Punish them with the rod and save them from death.*

God is speaking to us as parents, urging us to trust Him and have confidence in His Word; He exhorts us to discipline our children when their ways are not in alignment with the laws and principles of Jesus.

Eli knew what his children were doing in the Holy Temple of the Lord. He was a servant of God's law and teachings, yet he left his sons to do what they wanted. We know the story. He and his sons and their families' future came to an abrupt end. Death entered their household.

Eli's story is a call to us today. The consequences of neglect are extreme and very sad indeed. None of us want our families to end up in a situation like his. God loves us all so much. His love is unconditional. When the children that He loves and care for are living a sinful life, it grieves the heart of God. Because of the love He has for us, God the Father warns and disciplines us, the ones He loves. He is a true Father who loves us too much to refrain from intervening.

As we share the Father's heart, let us be aware of distractions. This is a constant challenge in our world. So many people have the habit of waking up and reaching for their mobile phones. We can easily spend so much time watching our favorite shows or seeking entertainment, idling away the hours rather than choosing to spend quality time in the secret place of the Most High God. Some people are simply so weary from the activities of life that they do not have the energy to devote five minutes of their time to praying for the needs of their families and others.

Let's not let these distractions keep us from fulfilling our role as watch-people over our families. We are going through a tough season right now. Satan loves to rob us of our time to intervene and engage with our children. How often do become carried away on technology, until suddenly we realize we've been distracted for hours? How does this happen? Satan is active in his quest to remove our focus from the Word and presence of God. He will use any means necessary to distract our minds from hearing the Lord's voice. He is a liar, manipulator and deceiver. We must be attentive and sensitive to the Spirit, staying alert and always maintaining our focus upon Jesus and the promises in His Word.

In Deuteronomy 28:1-2 we read,

> *If you diligently obey the voice of LORD your God, to observe carefully all His commandments . . . blessings shall come upon you and overtake you, because you obey the voice of the LORD your God.*

The word 'obey' means not merely to hear God's voice but also to submit to doing what He says. We must use our time wisely to meditate on the Word, presenting our praise and worship to our Heavenly Father. The more we spend time in God's presence, the clearer we can see and hear in the Spirit. Let's operate with a strong and discerning spirit, remaining sensitive to the voice and leading of the Spirit of God in our lives as we guide our precious families.

OTHERS DEPEND ON OUR LEADERSHIP

As we perform the important role of a watch-person in our families, churches, and communities, the members of our households and those around us are observing what we do. Those under our care and leadership respond to how we live our lives, and when our behavior matches what we preach and teach, they will more easily follow our lead. Our children watch our every action and look to us for their example. What a joy it is to know that as we live out our hope and purpose before them, we can guide their tender hearts to a strong faith in Jesus. As watchmen and heads of our households, we must manage the affairs of our families well, according to the ways and laws of God.

> *If anyone does not know how to manage his own family; how can he take care of God's church? . . . He must also have a good reputation with outsiders, so that he will not fall into disgrace and into the devil's trap.*
>
> **1 Timothy 3:5-7 (NIV)**

When we faithfully keep watch over our families, God can entrust us with the task of leading His people. Congregations look to their leaders; they follow our godly example. The people of the church want to witness and learn from spiritual mentors who work and live according to what they preach. They will learn to rise up in their own authority when they feel safe and secure—as their spiritual leaders guide them in the ways of God.

As pastors and leaders, we must faithfully serve Jesus and His people with love, remaining on guard as those who are entrusted to protect and look after the needs of the people. The Bible says that leaders or elders who do their work well are to be considered, "worthy of double honor, especially those who work hard at preaching and teaching" (1 Timothy 5:17 NIV). Therefore, as watchmen in the church, may we exercise our responsibility with an alert and focused mind, and with a spirit of faithfulness, love, respect, and honor.

The culture of the world around us is not getting any easier. We are living in times where many people struggle financially, mentally, and emotionally. With the outbreak of a global pandemic, much of the world has had to adjust to government-imposed restrictions, and many have been confined to their homes. What a perfect opportunity this is for Christians to stand as watch-people in our families, communities and nations, and to be on our knees in prayer, focused upon Jesus and cultivating an intimate relationship with the Holy Spirit.

> *Nevertheless I tell you the truth. It is to your advantage that I go away; for if I do not go away, the Helper will not come to you; but if I depart, I will send Him to you.*
>
> **John 16:7**

We are living in a season of the Holy Spirit! If you lack godly wisdom or the confidence to live and perform your responsibilities as a mighty watchperson in your family, just ask the Holy Spirit in Jesus' name! The Holy Spirit is our Counsellor—the One who can guide us to become strong, powerful and faithful watch-people who bring glory to Jesus! With Him as our Helper, let us press on to do our own part with obedience and let the Spirit of God do the rest. *Glory and honor to God Almighty!*

Dear God, thank You for calling us to become watchmen and watchwomen in our homes, churches, and nations. We declare that in the name of Jesus we are more than overcomers. We thank You, Holy Spirit, for the gift of discernment within us. We continue to trust in Your leading as we remain faithful in prayer while fixing our eyes upon Jesus' victory on the cross, and His resurrection power and glory. In Jesus' Name, Amen!

- Chapter Three -

REKINDLE THE LAMP IN YOUR HOME

As children of the heavenly Father, our spiritual ears need to be attentive at all times to the truth of the Good News. In the same way the body yearns for food, our spirits long for spiritual sustenance from Jesus and His Word.

Isaiah 26:20-21 says,

> *Come, my people, enter your chambers, and shut your doors behind you; Hide yourself, as it were, for a little moment, until the indignation is past. For behold, the Lord comes out of His place to punish the inhabitants of the earth for their iniquity; the earth will also disclose her blood, and will no more cover her slain.*

We are in an era where many different teachings about the Gospel of Jesus are delivered every day through social media and streaming platforms. We need to find sources that are appropriate, life-giving, and satisfying to our personal spiritual hunger.

I want to encourage you around the idea of *rekindling the lamp within your house*. Though this became more urgent during the season of Covid-19 lockdowns, it is appropriate in every generation. Gatherings and fellowships inside the churches are being limited and restricted. Laws have been passed which individuals and religious organizations must comply with. This is often for our safety. But when we are required to remain in our houses, let us ensure there is "light in our dwellings" (Exodus 10:23). This is a season in which we must rekindle the lamps in our homes! Jesus said,

> *You are the light of the world. A town built on a hill cannot be hidden. Neither do people light a lamp and put it under a bowl. Instead they put it on its stand, and it gives light to everyone in the house. In the same way, let your light shine before others, that they may see your good deeds and glorify your Father in heaven.*
>
> ***Matthew 5:14-16 (NIV)***

A lamp is a source of light that brightens a room, making an environment easier to navigate, and bringing details into clear view. Lamps bring light to any area that is covered with darkness—and they symbolize those of us who are believers.

Jesus is the light of the world. He Himself is our source of light and in turn, we bring light to the world. Jesus called *every* believer a lamp. He wants us to reflect His light, sharing it with others and bringing blessings to the lost world. Every good deed that we perform glorifies our Heavenly Father. We are His lamps!

In our current season, many people are fearful, not knowing where the road leads. What will be the outcome of the coronavirus? What does the future hold? Their hearts are unsettled, their minds battle with anxiety and helplessness, and perhaps there is even a spirit of unbelief towards Jesus' words and promises. As those who belong to God, His Word is our refuge. I encourage you, spend more time than ever in God's Word. Learn how to master your emotions and insecurities. Place your trust entirely in Him. God's plan is often not what we expect.

> *Come, my people, enter your chambers, and shut your doors behind you.*
>
> **Isaiah 26:20**

God clearly told His people to go and enter their chambers. Perhaps they did not know why, but *He* could clearly see what lay before them, even if they could not. God's plans are truly higher and greater than ours, and He can see further and more clearly than we can.

The Lord is explicitly telling us in this season to go into our rooms and shut the doors. God want us to get into the realm of the Spirit, our safest dwelling place. He is directing our steps to seek Him. He wants His children to remain in fellowship with Him through His Holy Word, prayer, praise and worship. As we find Him in the hidden place, He brings us under His protection and safety.

Allow me to share a personal revelation that has significantly transformed my own way of life. I feel like God is telling me, as His son who honors and obeys Him, that this is my season to stay still, trust Him, and enjoy His presence and blessings. It is as if He is sharing a divine secret—letting me know that there is a time and a season for everything that happens. Do you sense this too? Sons and daughters of God, *open your spiritual eyes* and embrace the opportunity of these days. This is not a time for complaint! The Bible foretold much of what the world is facing right now, therefore we can approach this season with confidence, knowing that God is not taken by surprise.

The truth is, our mighty and awesome God is inviting us to remain inside our homes and to lock ourselves deeper in His glorious presence, not only for our safety, but to bring us greater intimacy with Him. Though the wicked have good reason to fear, no trouble will come near us as we take refuge in Him.

Our houses are sanctified, covered with His powerful blood. Let us simply shut the doors, relax in His peace, and enjoy His perfect divine protection and provision during these trials. The world has long challenged the patience of God and taken His grace for granted. Now, as in the days when the Israelites were commanded to stay in their homes as the angel of the Lord passed over, let us trust in His purposes, knowing that God has us in His hand. Our heavenly Father wants us to enjoy peace, protection and provision.

The Spirit of God gave me a warning about preparing for the days ahead. He wants His children to be prepared to enter our rooms and shut the doors. We must not be spiritually laid back. We must constantly rekindle the spiritual lamp within our homes, assured that the God we serve and believe in is so wise! His plans are only to prosper and bless us (Jeremiah 29:11). *Hallelujah!*

A LIFE THAT PLEASES GOD

It is concerning to see that way in which the world around us has embraced ways of living that displease God. Sin and strife, wars and violence, permeate every culture on earth. God grieves over it all, but He also hates hypocrisy. When His people embrace lifestyles that are contrary to His Word it is an abomination to Him and heartbreaking to those who care for His people. The same is true for nations who remove God from their constitutions and institutions—and in families where people are caught up with hatred and unforgiveness. Around the world, there is an uprising of persecution against those who follow God and seek to live holy lives.

The Bible tells us that God loves us, but it also tells us that God hates sin. He is holy, just and righteous. When He sees those He created in His own special image living in disobedience to His will and commandments, it grieves His heart. There comes a time when His grace is exhausted—when rebellion has gone too far. At that point, Scripture tells us, God hands people over to their own desires (Romans 1). But what the devil means for evil, God will always use to restore His people! This is why He disciplines us and brings correction—so that we may live!

DISCOVER THE SECRET PLACE

Spiritual attacks are another reason that the flame in our lamps die out. We need to guard the joy of the Lord within us so we can resist the enemy's advances. As we pass through trials, we need the joy of Lord to spur us on, to give us strength while we seek Him diligently for His divine peace and protection upon our families. It is time to enter our rooms, shut the door and rekindle the spiritual lamps inside our homes until our lives overflow with the joy of the Lord, even in this season.

> *But you, when you pray, go into your room, and when you have shut your door, pray to your Father who is in the secret place; and your Father who sees in secret will reward you openly.*
>
> *Matthew 6:6*

My brothers and sisters in Christ, it is a good thing that God is doing for us at this time. Obey His instructions, gather your families, and rekindle the lamps inside your homes.

Lock your doors and pray secretly to our heavenly Father. Meditate on God's Word. Pray in the Spirit. Speak in tongues. Get intimate with Jesus through thanksgiving and worship. Praise Him with your loved ones, and sing hymns and psalms to the Lord. Discover God's secret place. There we will enjoy His presence, favor and protection, and see His plans come to pass. Gather your families and children, allow the Holy Spirit to guide you into the presence of the Father, and remain still in His peace and comfort.

THE JOY OF THE LORD

The joy of the Lord illuminates our lives as the oil of the Holy Spirit flows in us. There can be no flame or light without the oil. The oil and the anointing of the Holy Spirit are directly linked. Jesus' anointing upon believers is manifested in our lives as the Spirit of God performs and completes His works through His people.

You cannot enjoy God's presence, peace and provision without the anointing of the Spirit. It is the oil of the anointing that sustains our faith and joy in Jesus Christ! Joy is one of the fruits of the Holy Spirit (Galatians 5:22). Without it, our spiritual strength can deteriorate, the trials of this world can easily discourage us, and fear can overwhelm us. Joy is essential if we are to receive and appreciate God's blessing in our lives. Without joy, our spiritual lamp can easily burn out. Let us take time daily to seek afresh the regenerating presence and anointing of the Holy Spirit!

Faith to Believe

Faith is the essential element for a victorious spiritual life. It impacts every part of our being. It energizes us to press on during hardships, and it defends against the attack of the enemy. But faith is more than that. Through faith we survive—and even thrive—despite the problems and issues of life. Hebrews 11:6 says, "Without faith, it is impossible to please God." Jesus promised us the blessings and prosperity of Abraham. He gives us peace in times of trouble. He gives us hope and perseverance in times of suffering and pain. He gave us eternal life as a gift. Faith fuels *all* of these.

In order to maintain your lamp you must continue to have faith in Jesus. By faith, we can destroy all the evil works of the enemy against us. Continue to believe in Jesus' words of truth and life, and enjoy His divine peace and provision for you and your family, *by faith*.

Your lamp can only shine brightly as you live according to the ways of the Spirit of God. You can never overcome fear or difficult situations with your own strength or ability. Instead, you must build an intimate relationship with the Spirit of God through prayer, fasting, praise and worship, and meditation upon the Word of God. I tell you, friend, you will never reach your full potential and fulfil your purpose without the Spirit of God.

You are the light of the world, your oil will never run out, and your lamp will keep on burning and shining as long as you feed yourself spiritually. By faith, take hold of the weapons of the Spirit. We are fighting a war against the enemy, so we *cannot* lay back as if it were peacetime.

Enter the Throne Room

The apostle Paul exhorts us to pray without ceasing regardless of the season, whether in good times or bad. Prayer is a spiritual weapon. The Word of God is also a weapon—the spiritual sword that can foil Satan's evil schemes. It is the living water that refreshes our spirits. It is medicine for our bodies and souls. Study and meditate upon it, then use it to defend yourself and those you love. Prayer and fasting, praise and worship, will draw you closer to the throne-room of the Heavenly Father and activate His angels to work on your behalf.

God is a Spirit, and you and I are first and foremost spiritual beings, so we must live and work according to the principles and values of the spiritual realm. As we engage by faith with all we have available to us in the Spirit, we will be tireless and effective in the Kingdom of Jesus.

Shut the Door

After safely entering our houses, we need to make sure we shut the doors so that there is no gap for Satan to enter. We need to block every spiritual opening that could be a loophole for the devil to attack.

- Shut the door on negative and critical words that discourage you and your family.

- Shut the door on fear that comes against your faith.
- Shut the door on idolatry or mediocrity in your home.
- Shut the door on unforgiveness, hatred and jealousy.

When we shut the door on all the ways Satan seeks to gain a foothold, our families can triumph in Jesus' mighty name! Building and maintaining intimacy with Jesus is essential. We must do our part to spiritually foster our relationship with God, spend time meditating on His Word, teach and train our children about His ways, and prepare our households spiritually for the Lord's return. We, as the children of God, must yearn and desire for the presence of His Holy Spirit more than ever before.

Consider King David. I adore the heart of this man. He loved to dwell in the presence and house of God.

> *One thing I have desired of the Lord, that will I seek: That I may dwell in the house of the Lord all the days of my life, to behold the beauty of the Lord, and to inquire in His temple.*
>
> **Psalm 27:4**

What are you seeking during this season? Would you be like David, utterly focused in your desire for the Lord and His presence? David knew that this was his source of strength and courage. He knew that soaking in the Spirit and the glory of God was the secret to his victories in battle. Every time he faced an enemy army arrayed against him, he was aware of the glory of God surrounding him.

What about us? What are we really seeking? How much victory are we walking in? How much glory pervades our lives? In Isaiah 26:20, God calls us to come away with Him, to close our doors and hide ourselves for a moment "until the indignation is past." During this season, He invites us to meet with Him, to position our hearts towards Him as His end-time plans unfold.

Precious family of Christ, if you have strayed, take the opportunity to realign yourself in the will of God. This is a time to repent and secure your families, covering them with the blood of Jesus. Jesus' bride must take the time to prepare for His return, waiting in expectant faith for the coming of our glorious King. *Praise Jesus!*

So, rise up and rekindle your lamp. Gather your families and loved ones, build them up in the Spirit, develop and teach them with the Word and ways of God. Seek God's purpose for your life diligently, and rest in the divine peace and protection of Jesus. In this way, you will grow in strength and wisdom, truly able to serve our King Jesus, bringing honor and glory to the Father!

Dear Jesus, thank You for Your Word of truth. We declare that no trial or attack of the enemy may hinder our desire and love for You. We fan up the flame within, rekindling the lamp in us through Your Spirit and Holy Word. We confess that we can do the impossible, for You are our source of life and strength. Falling in love with You is the best decision that we ever made in life. We give You honor and glory. In Jesus mighty name we pray, Amen and Amen!

- Chapter Four -

LED BY THE SPIRIT

Jesus told His disciples that there would be a time when they would receive the Holy Spirit as their great Helper.

> *If you ask anything in My name, I will do it. If you love Me, keep My commandments. And I will pray to the Father, and He will give you another Helper, that He may abide with you forever—the Spirit of truth, whom the world cannot receive, because it neither sees Him nor knows Him, but you know Him, for He dwells with you and will be in you.*
>
> *John 14:14-17*

Jesus said to His disciples, "If you love me, keep my commandments" (v15). It was not only that He spent quality time with the disciples, performing miracles and exposing them to the wonders of His power. The Lord was also *teaching* and *equipping* His disciples for the work and will of His Heavenly Father, especially the works of the Holy Spirit. God's heart is for us to receive the Holy Spirit so that we might continue to perform His works on earth in His name.

THE PURPOSE OF THE HOLY SPIRIT

The purpose of the Holy Spirit is to help us continue the miraculous work of Jesus, to carry on His ministry on earth. Jesus ascended to heaven more than two thousand years ago, leaving the Holy Spirit to work and move within us that we may bring glory to Jesus. The Spirit of God also brings light to our souls—He reveals sin, truth, and the glory of Jesus. The people of the world rarely speak openly about the Holy Spirit. They don't know Him as we do.

Do you believe that the Holy Spirit lives within you? Do you honor and value Him? Do you allow Him to guide and lead you? Jesus said that the Holy Spirit is the Spirit of Truth. He is perfectly wise, with all understanding and power. As a believer, the Holy Spirit dwells in you and will be with you forever if you abide in Him. *Praise God!*

> *Jesus rejoiced in the Spirit and said, "I thank You, Father, Lord of heaven and earth, that You have hidden these things from the wise and prudent and revealed them to babes."*
>
> *Luke 10:21*

In this Scripture, Jesus was giving thanks in the Spirit to His Heavenly Father. He knew the gift of the Holy Spirit would reveal the secrets of His Kingdom to the meek and the lowly, allowing them to walk in even more knowledge than the wisest people of this world. 1 Corinthians 1:27 says, "But God has chosen the foolish things of the world to put to shame the wise, and God has chosen the weak things of the world to put to shame the things which are mighty." God's ways and order are not the same as the worldly system and structure. As we consider this, we are thankful and amazed. With this equipping, we can be used for His Kingdom and noble purposes. *Praise Jesus!*

God's Word is powerful and *living*. From our spiritual birth until we grow to maturity, we are dependent on His Word for our spiritual growth. While others may seek desperately for knowledge according to the ways and system of this world, we hunger for the things of the Spirit. As we abide in Him and allow Him to guide and lead us, the Holy Spirit reveals to us all the secrets of God's Kingdom.

As a person with a humble educational background who is now being used by God in mysterious ways, this is so encouraging to me. I never thought that one day God would use me to preach His Holy Word. I can confirm that God is faithful to perform His Word. *Glory to Jesus!* Trying to achieve the highest level of knowledge and expertise as possible is very healthy, but God's plan for His people is so much greater than any knowledge this world can give. *Hallelujah!*

Receive the Holy Spirit's Power

Before Jesus ascended to Heaven, He told His disciples to wait until the Holy Spirit came upon them, because He would be the source of their power.

> *And He said to them, "It is not for you to know times or seasons which the Father has put in His own authority. But you shall receive power when the Holy Spirit has come upon you; and you shall be witnesses to Me in Jerusalem, and in all Judea and Samaria, and to the end of the earth."*
>
> *Acts 1:7-8*

The Holy Spirit can discern all things. He can see through all the schemes of the evil one. He understands our strengths and our abilities, as well as our shortcomings and weaknesses, and He has the wisdom to weave it all together as He guides us forward.

In our journey as Christians, we often desire power but shrink back from pursuing a relationship with the Holy Spirit. Jesus made it very clear that we must receive the Holy Spirit first, then His power will come upon us. I urge you, my brothers and sisters in Christ, yearn for the Holy Spirit, for He is our spiritual force and source. The Holy Spirit supplies the anointing and power to perform miracles and to fulfil the calling of Jesus on our lives. The Holy Spirit remains in us to complete the mission of Jesus on earth. As we seek intimacy with Him, we are invited into that glorious work.

Jesus wants us to be His witness into the ends of the world. The Holy Spirit is our only source of strength, power and authority to accomplish this mission. He is our Helper, Comforter and Counsellor in times of needs. He gives the knowledge and wisdom we need to share His Gospel, perform miracles, heal, cast out demons, or set captives free! As a believer in Jesus, I assure you, through the ministry of the Holy Spirit, His anointing and power will be upon you as you perform the work of the Kingdom on earth.

Romans 8:14 says that those who are led by the Spirit of God are the sons (and daughters) of God.

He leads us. The opinion of pastors, family, or friends, even those with qualifications, wealth and status, fades in comparison. Through His influence, you will know the heart and will of God, and grow as a son or daughter who belongs in the Father's presence. Only a genuine son or daughter truly understands the heart of a father or mother. Children of God, I urge you, allow the Spirit of God to be your teacher, for this is the will of Jesus for us.

> *For you did not receive the spirit of bondage again to fear, but you received the Spirit of adoption by whom we cry out, "Abba, Father."*
>
> ***Romans 8:15***

The Holy Spirit brings freedom! You cannot be a slave to fear with the Holy Spirit living within you. You cannot be a child of God and remain in bondage. As His adopted sons and daughters, we will receive His inheritance as we allow the Holy Spirit to lead us and dwell in us. *Thank You, Father!*

HOW DOES THE HOLY SPIRIT LEAD US?

The Holy Spirit works through direct communication with our born-again spirit (John 4:24). He reveals the truth and glory of Jesus. He works through the areas of our lives that need development. The way we speak, think, act and behave, will all be slowly but surely transformed until we live a life of obedience to His Word of truth. He develops godly wisdom and understanding in us. He shows us how to make wise decisions that align with the will of Jesus in our lives. He directs our path by helping us to live a life that exudes the fruits of love, joy, peace, patience, kindness, goodness, faithfulness, gentleness, and self-control (Galatians 5:22).

The Holy Spirit's ministry is especially valuable in times of trials. He directs us to Jesus' divine peace, and trains us to be bold and faithful against all odds. He brings the anointing and power that enables us to perform the work of Jesus in spite of difficult circumstances, revealing God's glory in our lives.

As you allow the Holy Spirit to lead you in all your ways, your vision will become clear, you will become familiar with God's voice, and you will diligently live out His will with joy and peace. *Thank You, Holy Spirit!*

The Seal of the Holy Spirit

What a joy to know that God has *already* put His seal upon us—the seal and confirmation of our faith, the promise and pledge that He will complete His Word in us at the moment of salvation and that our future is safeguarded. A formal seal is a an individually designed stamp, usually made from wax, which guarantees the authenticity of the document to which it is applied. In its simplest form, it functions as a 'legal signature,' confirming ownership or validating whatever is sealed.

The Holy Spirit stamped and sealed you as His own from the moment of your spiritual birth. This is surely a confirmation that we belong to Jesus—the Holy Spirit is a mark of adoption upon us as believers, and a guarantee for eternal future and inheritance in Jesus Christ our Lord and King. *Praise the Lord!*

> *In Him you also trusted, after you heard the word of truth, the gospel of your salvation; in whom also, having believed, you were sealed with the Holy Spirit of promise.*
>
> **Ephesians 1:13**

Since you have already been sealed by the Holy Spirit, you belong to Jesus. The works of the Holy Spirit have been revealed and confirmed in your life, just as He promised! Having ascended to heaven, Jesus is seated at the right hand of the Father. Everything that we want to do in this world calls upon the divine connection between the Holy Spirit and Jesus and the Father in heaven. The gospel of

John explains it like this:

> *However, when He, the Spirit of truth, has come, He will guide you into all truth; for He will not speak on His own authority, but whatever He hears He will speak; and He will tell you things to come. He will glorify Me, for He will take of what is Mine and declare it to you. All things that the Father has are Mine. Therefore I said that He will take of Mine and declare it to you.*
>
> *John 16:13-15*

Isn't it amazing how close the relationship is between the Holy Spirit, Jesus and the Father? The Trinity operates in unity. It is this intimacy with heaven that confirms the work of the Holy Spirit in our lives. Everything that God the Father wants to reveal to us comes through Jesus and the Holy Spirit who communicates to us in many ways, including through dreams and revelations, or *'rhema'* words of spoken instruction into our spirits. When we receive a revelation from God and allow the Holy Spirit to lead, He will move within us to bring that word to pass. Everything the Father has belongs to Jesus, and through the Holy Spirit, it is made available to us.

How blessed we are to have the Holy Spirit! Without Him, we could never complete our calling. He has revealed the secrets of His Kingdom to us. Those who are caught up in a worldly perspective cannot understand Him, but as His children we believe and enter into fulness through Him. We are 'People of the Spirit' in this world! We are sealed with the Holy Spirit and belong to Jesus alone!

How is your relationship with the Holy Spirit? A relationship with Him is life-giving and intimate, but we must also take care that we do not grieve Him.

> *And do not grieve the Holy Spirit of God, by whom you were sealed for the day of redemption.*
>
> **Ephesians 4:30**

The Holy Spirit has a will and a personality. This means He can be offended! To grieve Him means to cause Him sadness, sorrow, pain of distress. Let's not rebel against the work of the Spirit, or even speak against His power and presence by our words or actions. Romans 8:9-17 says,

> *But you are not in the flesh but in the Spirit, if indeed the Spirit of God dwells in you. Now if anyone does not have the Spirit of Christ, he is not His. And if Christ is in you, the body is dead because of sin, but the Spirit is life because of righteousness. But if the Spirit of Him who raised Jesus from the dead dwells in you, He who raised Christ from the dead will also give life to your mortal bodies through His Spirit who dwells in you. Therefore, brethren, we are debtors—not to the flesh, to live according to the flesh. For if you live according to the flesh you will die; but if by the Spirit you put to death the deeds of the body, you will live. For as many as are led by the Spirit of God, these are sons of God. For you did not receive the spirit of bondage again to fear, but you received the Spirit of adoption by whom we cry out, "Abba, Father." The Spirit Himself bears witness*

> *with our spirit that we are children of God, and if children, then heirs—heirs of God and joint heirs with Christ, if indeed we suffer with Him, that we may also be glorified together.*

We are being made glorious! This means that our flesh should no longer triumph. His Spirit is strong in us. With the Word of God dwelling in us, it is easier for our flesh to diminish, submitting to the voice of the Spirit in us. God is holy. Our body is the temple of the Holy Spirit (1 Corinthians 6:19). Therefore, everything that we do in our bodies must be holy, pleasing to God rather than grieving Him. By His Spirit we overcome the works of the flesh—adultery, hatred, anger, idolatry, unforgiveness, gossip, sexual immorality, drunkenness and so on.

Every time we yield and submit to sin and desires of the flesh, we grieve the Holy Spirit. But the One who is most affected by our lapses into sin is also the One who brings us freedom from it! Let's continue to obey the voice of the Holy Spirit, crucifying our flesh, and welcoming the presence of the Holy Spirit, who brings blessing and joy to our lives, and enables us to please the heart of the Heavenly Father.

I urge you all brothers and sisters in Christ, desire to receive the Holy Spirit. Allow Him to guide and lead you in all your ways and plans. He is our source of strength, the divine light that reveals the truth and glory of Jesus in our lives. With Him indwelling us, we can joyfully undertake the assignment and calling of Jesus in this world. May you be blessed as you freely allow the Holy Spirit to lead you in all your plans and decisions!

Dear Jesus, we thank You so much for Your Holy Spirit. You are our great helper, counsellor, advocate, leader, divine light and truth. We declare that without Your Holy Spirit we can never truly please Your heart and bring glory to Your name. Help us mend our ways of living and submit to the wisdom and power of Your Spirit so that we will continue to become stronger and greater in doing Your will. We thank You, Holy Spirit, for greater are You in us, than Satan and his forces in this world. We bless Your name, Lord Jesus, Amen!

- Chapter Five -

HOLD ONTO THE VISION

Vision is divine revelation, the ability to 'see' the future with our spiritual imagination. The word 'vision' is mentioned often in the Bible. Throughout the Old Testament, we read of God's messengers and prophets holding onto vision as they waited for 'the fulness of time,' the moment when God ordained the vision to be fulfilled. Now, more than two thousand years ago after Jesus ascended to heaven, we can see how many of those revelations and visions spoken through God's prophets have been fulfilled, just as God had spoken.

> *I will stand my watch, and set myself on the rampart, and watch to see what He will say to me, and what I will answer when I am corrected. Then the LORD answered*

> me and said: *"Write the vision down and make it plain on tablets, that he may run who reads it. For the vision is yet for an appointed time; but at the end it will speak, and it will not lie. Though it tarries, wait for it; Because it will surely come, it will not tarry."*
>
> *Habakkuk 2:1-3*

It is the same with the vision God places within us. Every man-made creation started with vision. In fact, everything about our everyday lives originates from a vision. The houses that we live in began as a vision in the mind of an architect or builder. The car that you drive was first invented in somebody's vision. The clothes, toiletries, accessories, groceries, technology, forms of transportations, railroads, motorways and highways all began as a vision which has now been fulfilled!

In simple words, the whole world and its surroundings were invented from the power of a *revelation* or a *vision*. What God can create via the human brain, through the knowledge and potential of the world's most qualified professors, experts and scientists, to form and build all these man-made creations for humankind, is amazing! We too are created beings, the product of divine vision. We were conceived in the heart and mind of the Trinity! There is a divine connection between us and God Almighty.

Abraham was a man who carried a vision in his heart. God spoke to Abraham to leave his father's house and all his extended relatives, taking his wife and servants to a place where He would lead them. Abraham did not know where that would be, and when God spoke, He did not give details to Abraham about how long it would take or what would happen on the journey ahead. But as soon as Abraham heard God's voice, he took it as a divine revelation from God. All he could do was to trust God. And so, he rose up and followed his vision until he reached his final destination!

When God speaks to you about something, it doesn't necessarily mean it will happen immediately. It's the same when God delivers instructions to any servant, prophet, or minister within the church. Everything that He wants to reveal comes with a certain timeframe in which God will bring it to pass. The pastor, therefore, needs to write down the revelation, pray about it, hold onto the vision with persistence, and wait upon God to fulfil the vision in its appointed time.

In the Bible, everything commanded by God happens according to His will. It is similar to how we structure a business or company. In every organization, there is a vision. This vision, which each member of the company focusses on, helps them to achieve their goals, whether individually or as a team. Likewise, in our churches we must have a God-given vision that allows us to fulfil the calling of God and live out our purpose on earth.

WRITE THE VISION

What does it mean to write down the vision and keep it? In my interpretation, it means that whatever vision God gives you, write it down *in your heart* and keep it there until it comes to pass. Don't leave the vision in your mind, because the human mind is a battlefield of Satan; he will snatch it from you. Your vision needs to be transferred *to your heart*. Be vigilant to preserve the vision God gives you! You must receive with eyes of the Spirit, and immediately place it deeply inside your heart, guarding it well until its due time.

Daniel 7:1-28 speaks about specific dreams and visions that God gave Daniel. In response, Daniel literally wrote everything down and followed through as instructed. He also carried the vision in his heart. Some of the events of Daniel's vision about the end times are only fulfilled in the book of Revelation—we are still waiting for God's timing to come to pass!

I find that, if I do not write a vision down, I easily forget it. Once a vision is written, however, it enters your heart; it is easy to remember and retrieve at any time. Staying curious about how the vision will be outworked will make you excited, and seeing the vision in writing helps us to keep pressing on and walking towards it until it is completed. When that vision is accomplished in the timing and will of God, it will not only positively influence others but many souls that are lost without Jesus will be transformed and changed for the better.

> *For whatever things were written before were written for our learning, that we through the patience and comfort of the Scriptures might have hope.*
>
> ***Romans 15:4***

At the very beginning of time, a promise was given that a son would be born and that He would crush the head of Satan. God fulfilled this prophesy when He sent Jesus into the world more than two thousand years ago. Thus, whatever is written in the Word of God is for our instruction, learning and discipline, to have hope and trust in God that He will perform His Word of truth in His own perfect time.

What is written in the Scriptures helps us hold onto vision so that we can continue to have hope even as we wait for the fulfillment of God's promises. One of the glorious reasons for hope in our generation is the coming of Jesus Christ. This has been foretold and prophesied years ago; even the wickedness, pain, suffering, trials and hardships we face in these days were written about in the Bible a long time ago. The Word of God is still speaking to us in this day and age, helping us to lay hold of hope and patiently wait for the Lord's return. Amen!

I encourage you brothers and sisters in Christ, no matter how many hardships we face, our living hope is in Jesus and in His Word.

> *Beloved, do not forget this one thing, that with the Lord one day is as a thousand years, and a thousand years as one day. The Lord is not slack concerning His promise, as some count slackness, but is longsuffering toward us, not willing that any should perish but that all should come to repentance.*
>
> **2 Peter 3:8-9**

I urge you, whatever vision God gives you for your life, family or church, write it down and keep it in your heart. Seek God diligently and wait patiently upon Him. If God has spoken to you that you will become an evangelist, pastor, teacher, prophet, or apostle, you must seek divine guidance from the Holy Spirit through prayer, mediation on His Word, worship, and fasting until you see it come to pass. Perhaps He has given you a vision or a revelation to be a business owner. Others are being called as artists or musicians. This is for His glory! Meditate on His Word, write down the lyrics, tune into His pictures and songs, and seek Him diligently for the kind of art or music and worship that pleases His heart and moves heaven.

> *Those who wait upon the Lord shall renew their strength; they shall mount up with wings like eagles, they shall run and not be weary, they shall walk and not faint.*
>
> **Isaiah 40:31**

VISIONS ARE FOR YOUNG AND OLD

Visions are for everyone, even the young. Truly, a vision or a revelation can be given to any age group.

> *And it shall come to pass in the last days, says God, that I will pour out of My Spirit on all flesh; Your sons and your daughters shall prophesy, your young men shall see visions, your old men shall dream dreams.*
>
> **Acts 2:17**

God can give the vision to anyone that He desires, and so all of us, whatever our age or situation, are obliged to seek Him diligently for divine vision. God is not a respecter of men; everyone is the same in His eyes. God will pour His Spirit upon our young sons and daughters; they will prophesy and see visions, just as old men and women will dream and receive revelations as well.

If you are a youth or a young adult, you *must* know that you are very special to the plan of God. You must rise up and allow the Holy Spirit to anoint and guide you as you seek God's will for your life. If God says that you will see visions, you must believe it. Open your ears to hear His voice and wait upon Him as He fulfils your destiny. The Spirt of God will lead you until that vision is performed in your life. God has poured out His grace on you! As the young generation, do not imitate and replicate the lifestyles of this world. There are many divine visions that God wants to reveal to you that will bless your life and give glory to Jesus. God wants to use your strength mightily for His Kingdom.

Joseph is a great example of a boy to whom God gave revelation of future events and occurrences from a young age. Those dreams and visions started to be fulfilled in his own household. Then his brothers got jealous of him and abandoned and sold him to Egyptians. Later, when he was working with integrity and honesty in Potiphar's household, he was accused of sexual harassment by the master's wife, but still Joseph's faith was firm in God and the visions that he saw. Because of the dreams and visions of his youth, Joseph knew that God had a plan in his life. He knew that one day his living God would come in mighty power and bless him.

Sometimes God allows tests like this to stretch our level of trust and faith in His plan. The Bible tells us that what Satan meant for evil, God wove into His master plan to bring prosperity to Joseph and salvation to his family during the famine, but most of all, to show His power and glory to King Pharaoh and his people. The end of this story is amazing. Joseph became second in charge next to Pharaoh—all because of the power of a dream and vision that God brought to pass for him. It blessed him and his family, but also brought glory and honor to God Almighty!

Samuel is another example of young boy that God communicated with through a vision. He too went through a waiting process. At a very young age, God called him and trained him through Eli to hear His voice and learn His ways and His principles. Samuel served Eli faithfully while waiting upon God's time to fulfil His vision upon his life. He became the greatest prophet of Israel, and God's most trusted and loyal prophet used to protect His nation.

Lastly, let's consider Noah. God spoke to Noah that He intended to destroy the wicked and disobedient human race by sending a flood. But He had mercy in His heart. Finding Noah to be righteous, He gave him a vision of what to do to save his family, laying down detailed instructions regarding the dimensions of the ark and how the animals and their kinds should be sorted in pairs to bring into the ark.

When God gives you a vision, you may be the only one who knows exactly how God lays down the instruction, plan, steps and the order, until that vision is fulfilled! But take heart—it is for your blessing and for the blessing of those you love. *Amen!*

Noah's vision from God saved his family. Many times, he urged and cried out to the people to repent from their sins, to turn away from their wicked ways and listen to God. Yet they mocked him, criticized him, laughed at him and called him a crazy old man for building this gigantic ark on dry land. Only Noah's children and his wife supported his vision and trusted God's plan. Sadly, when God's timing was up and the vision was fulfilled, He sent the flood and everyone died—except for Noah and his household. What a mighty God we serve! He honors divine vision and revelation, showing His power and glory as He brings blessing to His people. *Glory to God!*

THE TIMING OF THE VISION

Once you confirm your calling from God, wait upon Him patiently until it is His time. God is never too early or too late to help us. When He gives a vision, He always keeps His promise and brings it to pass at His own pace, not only for our own benefit, but to bring glory to His name. God said He will give us inner strength if we wait patiently upon Him. We will mount on wings and soar like eagles if we trust Him and have faith in His timing.

This is important because through our journey in life we are often quick to receive divine vision, but impatient to seek God and wait upon His timing. Our natural instinct is to follow through immediately, rather than seek out God and allow the Holy Spirit to lead us, waiting for confirmation from God. It is important to understand that in God's divine order there is always a seeking period through consistent prayers and fasting, meditating on His Word, learning, and waiting. We will only reach our final destination when we pass the test of faithfulness!

So, seek Him diligently and wait patiently upon Him. Trust His timing for He knows what is dangerous, and He knows what is good for us. He is not slack concerning His promises; in God's timing, one day is the same a thousand years. You must seek His leading and guidance first, waiting upon Him with endurance for time to be right that He will fulfil that vision in you. *Hallelujah!*

Scripture reinforces the idea that vision will be fulfilled or will come to pass in God's timing.

> *Now as they came down from the mountain, Jesus commanded them, saying, "Tell the vision to no one until the Son of Man is risen from the dead."*
>
> ***Matthew 17:9***

> *Then Jesus said to them, "My time has not yet come, but your time is always ready . . . I am not yet going up to this feast, for My time has not yet fully come."*
>
> ***John 7:6-8***

This vision is for a future time. It describes the end, and it will be fulfilled. If it seems slow in coming, wait patiently, for it will surely take place. It will not be delayed.

Habakkuk 2:3 (NLT)

Therefore, do not go on passing judgment before the time, but wait until the Lord comes who will both bring to light the things hidden in the darkness and disclose the motives of men's hearts; and then each man's praise will come to him from God.

1 Corinthians 4:5 (NASB, 1995)

TRUST GOD WITH THE VISION

We can see that God's timing is different from our own ways of doing things. You can be sure that, when He gives you a certain assignment, He knows the risk, the conditions of your circumstances, and the shortcomings in your life that need to be addressed before you can be ready to receive it. Consider God's ways of doing things. Men and women of this world will always bring pressure and distress to discourage you. People will criticize the visions and dreams in you but if you hold firm to what God has given to you and guard it well with all your heart, nothing will be able to keep you from God's plans and blessings. If you try to outwork the vision in your own pace and timing, I tell you, chaos will come upon you and God's plan and desire to prosper you will be delayed in your life. Don't listen to the wrong voices, or those who drag you down. Know that God gave you a vision for a divine purpose, and your job is to hold firm to it and keep on trusting Jesus until you see it.

Surrender your own desires and plans, and obediently follow the leading of the Holy Spirit. It is only through the anointing and power of the Spirit of God in you that you can accomplish your God-given assignment. Once you hear from Jesus, simply follow His instructions, and adjust your ways of living to align with the teaching of His Word.

The Fulfillment of the Vision

You will know in the end that your vision is from God when the answers to your prayers are being fulfilled. Often, we want to rush things to serve our own desires, but Jesus knows the danger and the risk of our own mindset and flesh. Therefore, do not lean not on your own understanding or look to your physical circumstances, but trust the Lord's guidance with all your heart. If you do that, He will direct and guide you on straight paths that will accomplish your vision (Proverbs 3:5-6). If the vision is of God, He will never come too early, or show up late to perform it. The Word of Jesus is truth, and He always keeps His promise. *Hallelujah, Lord Jesus!*

Children of God, I urge you again, people may not believe in you, especially when God gives you an unusual vision that the natural mind cannot comprehend. But understand that God's thoughts and ways are higher than our own. He is God Almighty, holy and just. When He speaks to you and instructs you to do something, I encourage you, write down the vision in your heart. Hold firm to it, seek Him through the leading of His Holy Spirit, and accept training and discipline until your faith grows deeper. Wait patiently upon Jesus until He fulfils that vision in you. God is never too early, and He is not slack concerning His promises. God's timing is perfect and we will be satisfied. He said that in the last days, He would pour out His Spirit upon us all. May the Lord Jesus bring all your visions and dreams to pass, not only to bless your life and others, but most of all, for His glory!

Dear God, today we hear Your Word and we ask for Your guidance, wisdom and understanding to direct us into our final destination. We declare that every divine vision that You have given to us we will hold firm onto and keep in our hearts, waiting upon You patiently until You bring them to pass. You said in Your Word that You are not slack concerning Your promises. We thank You for Your divine plan and will in us. Glory to You Alone. In Jesus' Mighty name we pray, Amen!

- Chapter Six -

Faithfully Run your Race

In many seasons, I have watched through the eyes of my spirit how God's plans so often differ from that of humans. No wonder His Word tells us that God's ways are not the same as ours, that His thoughts are higher than ours (Isaiah 55:8-9).

During the lockdown season of the coronavirus pandemic, God revealed to my heart that we would emerge from that period as strong spiritual warriors of Jesus. Praise God! What an amazing opportunity to strengthen our faith in the Spirit and focus on Jesus' power, provision, and protection. We must not squander this season of our lives, lying back on our couches while we watch our favorite television programs. Satan is very smart and he knows exactly how to play with our minds and flesh. But when we recognize that God has given us time to seek Him and connect to the realm of the Spirit, we are encouraged. There is a great crowd of heavenly witnesses and saints looking on—a crowd who have completed their mission well on earth, and are now cheering for us and calling out to us to be strong and to take heart. *Amen!*

> *. . . Since we are surrounded by so great a cloud of witnesses, let us lay aside every weight, and the sin which so easily ensnares us, and let us run with endurance the race that is set before us, looking unto Jesus, the author and finisher of our faith, who for the joy that was set before Him endured the cross, despising the shame, and has sat down at the right hand of the throne of God.*
>
> ***Hebrews 12:1-2***

I want to ask you: How is your spiritual journey right now? How are you running your race for Jesus? How have you coped with the days of pandemic that have affected our world? The truth is, we should not waste time worrying and being lazy at home. Inspired by those who have gone before us and now cheer us on, let us trust the leading of the Holy Spirit to carry us, even in the tough seasons of life, so that we can finish our race well.

RUNNING TO WIN

When the author of Hebrews used the picture of a race, he wrote of the need to be faithful. Our Christian journey is like that of a runner who competes in a race with the aim of winning a prize. There is to be no breaking of the rules or plotting our own course! We must run in a faithful manner, worthy of achieving the reward. And, we must finish the course, remaining steadfast until the end.

As believers, our spiritual race is focused on one prize only—eternal life in Jesus Christ, our Lord and King. We run this race, not because the faithful warriors of God in the past made it successfully and were awarded with their glorious crown, but because Jesus excites and thrills our souls and He is our inheritance! *Glory to Jesus!*

The book of Hebrews depicts our Christian faith as a race that is to be run voluntarily, with joy . . . and yet we are to run with persistence. Why? Because there are things that can hinder us from finishing our race, issues that can drag us down and keep us from accomplishing our goal and receiving the final reward. That is why we must lay aside every weight and run our race of faith, not in our own physical strength, but courageously in the Spirit.

> *Brethren, I do not count myself to have apprehended; but one thing I do, forgetting those things which are behind and reaching forward to those things which are ahead.*
>
> ***Philippians 3:13***

When Paul wrote those words, was the apostle encouraging us to ignore our past? No—but he is encouraging us to leave behind all our old-self attitudes and behaviors, the things we enjoyed and idolized that contradict the will of Jesus. As 'new creations' who are now born-again Christians, every old habit including the lusts of the flesh and idols that we served, must be completely removed. We take our place on Jesus' race-track as runners who are unencumbered, persistent even in the face of trials or discouragement, and worthy of His Kingdom. The ways and rules of the race that Paul is talking about are based on the Word of God, not our own inclinations.

Paul knew that even as believers, if our past issues and sinful behaviors are not dealt with, they can become a hindrance, opening doors of discouragement and becoming a distraction that can rob our focus from Jesus and the eternal reward He has in store for us. As new creations in Christ, we cannot live according to the "lusts of the flesh" and run our race well for Jesus. As faith-runners, we must run in a manner that pleases Him.

What to Leave Behind

Let us look at some of the things that Paul says we must leave behind. As sons and daughters of God, the main purpose of our calling in this world is to spread the Gospel of Jesus, to seek and save the lost, heal the sick, cast out demons, and set the captives free, knowing that there is an eternal prize waiting for us. This is why we are not only encouraged to fix our eyes upon Jesus, but we are exhorted to lay aside every weight and sin that could hinder us from finishing our race faithfully.

Let me ask you: What are the heavy loads that slow you down and block your focus upon Jesus? Is sin and unfaithfulness in your life keeping you from finishing your race triumphantly? The apostle Peter wrote that we must, "lay aside all malice, all deceit, hypocrisy, envy, and all evil speaking" (1 Peter 2:1). He is alerting us to the fact that it is not only 'sins of the flesh' such as adultery, sexual immorality, murder, drunkenness, stealing and drug addictions, that we must leave behind, but sins of the *heart* as well.

Proverbs 4:23 says that we must keep our hearts with all diligence, because *from our hearts* spring all the issues of life. In the Kingdom of God, rewards are linked to faithfulness, and as such, our heart is of utmost importance. Sins of the heart are weighty—a jealous heart or spirit will never help us run our race. If our heart is full of envy, spite, and unclean and rival emotions, the Holy Spirit cannot abide there. We are the temple of the Holy Spirit, and He loves to dwell in a pure and clean heart. Therefore, we must cleanse our hearts at all times.

In Matthew 5:8, Jesus said, "Blessed are the pure in heart, for they shall see God." So let us keep our hearts pure, for this is the way we can see God the Father and be rewarded at the end of our race. Let's allow God to search our hearts as we faithfully serve in the calling and ministry He has entrusted to us, not performing for the eyes of men, but seeking only to please the Lord. God is not unfaithful—He will reward those whose hearts are truly His. In fact, the book of Revelation speaks of the final judgement as a time of prizegiving, a scene when we will be rewarded for the way we have conducted ourselves on earth. In our 'faith race,' our singleness of heart is essential to God. We must not be jealous of someone else's good deeds. If we have been wronged, we must leave an unforgiving spirit behind and replace it with a heart of forgiveness.

We must not only remove jealousy from our lives, but also deceitfulness. As believers we must serve God with truth and honesty, and not with lies and deception. We need to destroy the spirit of slander, hatred and anger that tries to hinder and block our focus on Jesus. As loyal and faithful servants who are focused upon Jesus, fulfilling His mission in our lives requires a heart that is humble, pure, holy, and obedient. We must walk with a positive mindset and a Christlike character. God desires to reward us according to our conduct; He alone searches our hearts.

1 Samuel 16:7 says that "man looks at the outside appearance, but God looks at the heart." In Acts 13:22 we read that God found a man after His own heart—David, the son of Jesse—who would do "all His will." What an example for us! *Praise God!*

I want to encourage you, wherever you are running your race, whether in your workplace, church ministry, or within your family, work with a pure and clean heart. Cleanse your heart and mind daily with the Word of God. The lifestyle and system of this world is not the same as a life that is transformed by the work of the Spirit of God.

And do not be conformed to this world, but be transformed by the renewing of your mind, that you may prove what is that good and acceptable and perfect will of God.

Romans 12:2

In his letter to Timothy, Paul writes particularly to those who are young, saying that we should flee from the things that weigh us down. Instead, he exhorts us to:

... pursue righteousness, godliness, faith, love, patience, gentleness. Fight the good fight of faith, lay hold on eternal life, to which you were also called and have confessed the good confession in the presence of many witnesses.

1 Timothy 6:11-12

Another weight we must lay aside is any evil talk and filthy words that come from our mouths. Sometimes, in wanting to be part of the crowd, we end up gossiping or discouraging our brothers and sisters in Christ. Folly and retaliatory language hurt others as they run their race. This is not pleasing in the eyes of God. Every time we sin with our mouths, our burden gets heavier to the point where we cannot move forward anymore.

But now you yourselves are to put off all these: anger, wrath, malice, blasphemy, filthy language out of your mouth.

Colossians 3:8

There's a common sin here that most of us Christians get caught with—anger. When we are angry, things around us end up in a chaos. In homes where anger is in a husband and wife's relationship, it always affects the children in the family. By the time your mind calms down, it can be too late to fix what has been broken—filthy language, cursing, and hurtful words spoken to each other have already touched the children. This can hinder their faith in Jesus, even while they desperately try with their fragile hearts to run their race for the eternal reward.

God knows that anger is part of our human nature. He created us with emotions, but His Word says we must not let anger linger—we must deal with it before the sun goes down (Ephesians 4:26). We must remember God's Word and quickly repent, release forgiveness, and amend everything according to His ways. I want to warn you, don't serve God with anger, because it will draw your attention away from winning your prize in Jesus.

The truth is, all of our words either bring life—or death. When we use language that demeans others or dishonors God, we become prone to weakness. We get slowed down in the race and are easily burned-out, losing our focus on Him. Let us not be those who, at the end of the race, are too weak to cross the finish line that Jesus set out for us. Psalm 55:22 says,

Cast your burden on the Lord, and He shall sustain you.

Peter also says that we can cast all our care on Him because He cares for us (1 Peter 5:7). He wants us to exchange our heavy burdens with Him, so that we can rest in His peace (Matthew 11:28). *Hallelujah Jesus!*

TRAINING TO RUN

God disciplines the ones He loves. In a family, there are moments when a father and mother sit down to discipline their children if they see them making mistakes or living unfaithfully. It's exactly the same with God. When we live in sin, God uses His Word of truth to correct and discipline us until we repent and walk in obedience.

We are living in a world where each one of us face different trials and tests—this is why there is a specific *rhema*, a spoken word from God that is appropriate for each of our situations. Even as a pastor, there are times when I have allowed a spirit of heaviness, anxiety, or worry to hinder my relationship with others and God. This strains my faith and delays me from running my spiritual race, but the moment the Spirit of God reminds me about the cloud of witnesses cheering me on and the reward of Jesus, I rise up again and continue on running accordingly to the leading of the Holy Spirit.

Let's keep looking up! Jesus desires a heart that repents and yields to His discipline and correction. God disciplines and corrects *those He loves*. The prize is eternal life! This end-reward is far too greater to compromise. Let us not miss it! I've said before that our battle is spiritual warfare. We are fighting and wrestling against Satan and his evil forces. The battle is daily so stay firm, and be obedient to the Word of

God. Being weighed down results in delay as God outworks His divine plan for our lives. Perhaps God wanted you to move in your faith long ago and is calling you to new level of blessings, but you may still be stuck due to stubbornness and disobedience. Take heart that He knows the full potential and ability in you; He desires to lift the level of your situation and circumstances, but these little issues hinder your faith while you run your race.

Perhaps you have got used to hearing only what makes you feel better. Be careful not to listen to the plea to forsake sin and seek the Lord, yet do nothing to grow spiritually. Our hearts can become hard when we turn to sugar-coated preaching that does not draw our focus back to Jesus. If we know our prize and reward is Jesus, let's keep our focus upon Him. Paul clearly says in Philippians 3:14, "I press toward the goal for the prize of the upward call of God in Christ Jesus."

Paul desired for us to run our race with the goal in mind. When we focus upon something, we put our full attention, mind and heart towards it. If you know that the prize for your race is Jesus, then do not compromise. Maintain your focus on Him by faith. Whatever Jesus commands us to do, let us obey and perform it with joy. Truly, the joy of the Lord is our strength! (Nehemiah 8:10, NLT).

Run with Patience

Running our race of faith is a long-term activity that requires perseverance, endurance, and inner-joy in order to sustain it. Although faithful men and women of God are cheering for us, we have our own race to run as individuals, and for that, we need a constant source of joy. That joy only comes when we meet our object of faith—Jesus. Let's commit to a life-long journey, keeping to the path that our Lord Jesus has already set out for us.

> *Thus says the Lord, your Redeemer, the Holy One of Israel: "I am the Lord your God, who teaches you to profit, who leads you by the way you should go."*
>
> **Isaiah 48:17**

If Jesus set out the path, marking the way so that we can finish the race, then we should believe Paul when he says that we can do all things through Jesus Christ who strengthens us (Philippians 4:13). We can trust Jesus wholeheartedly, for He is the perfect example of our faith. He is the victor, founder, and perfecter of our faith. He is our perfect example, the One who persevered and endured the cross because of the joy that was set before Him, and because of His unconditional love for us (Hebrews 12:2).

FOLLOW THE SPIRIT'S LEAD

To finish your race faithfully, you must depend on the Holy Spirit to lead you. Galatians 5:22 says that faithfulness is a fruit of the Holy Spirit. He is the One who enables us to run and not be weary. He cares about the motives of our hearts, not how much we do for Him. He is the One who comforts us and strengthens us, who keeps us from losing heart or becoming discouraged. As we cooperate with the Holy Spirit, He helps us to remove every weight, to leave the past behind, and to be transformed into a new creation in Jesus. By His grace we move forward and live in a way that pleases God until we reach our final destination. Let us focus our spiritual eyes upon Jesus alone and the eternal prize He has promised. May God bless you as you continue to run your race!

Heavenly Father, we thank You for Your precious Word that reminds us to serve You faithfully and continue running our race with joy, focusing our eyes upon Your Son, Jesus Christ. You have asked us to remove all the past habits and sins that hinder us from reaching our full potential for Christ. We trust and have faith in You, for You have appointed us to complete the work of Jesus here on earth as Your loyal servants. We thank You for the holy saints that are witnessing and cheering for us on our journey in life. We declare that heaven is our eternal home. We are looking forward to achieving the goal to which we are called, and receiving the prize that You promised for us in Christ Jesus. We love you, Father God. In the precious name of our Lord Jesus we pray, Amen!

- Chapter Seven -

DESTROYING GIANTS

The Word of God is not only a lamp to our feet and a light to our path—it is also effective for pulling down spiritual strongholds. With the Word of God as our weapon, we can come against every giant in our lives and in the lives of our families. First, we must be strengthened by it, healed, molded and equipped by the Word. When our inner-person is spiritually strong, we will never be shaken. But we must also learn to use the Word of God to bring down Satan and silence his taunts. *Praise the Lord!*

I have often said that the current season is not easy. Satan and His kingdom are invading our homes and families and playing around with our faith, trying to manipulate and deceive God's people. If we are not fully prepared and spiritually equipped, or do not understand the power and authority of the Word of God in our lives, we create a foothold for the enemy. The Bible tells us that Satan enters like a thief, seeking to destroy the peace and love in our homes. Regardless of what may be going on in the world around us, let us praise our Lord Jesus for His Holy Spirit who seals us and for His precious blood which shelters us from the attack of the enemy.

1 Samuel chapter 1 tells the story of David and Goliath—a story which is particularly encouraging in this season.

> *And the Philistine said to David, "Come to me, and I will give your flesh to the birds of the air and the beasts of the field!" Then David said to the Philistine, "You come to me with a sword, with a spear, and with a javelin. But I come to you in the name of the Lord of hosts, the God of the armies of Israel, whom you have defied. This day the Lord will deliver you into my hand, and I will strike you and take your head from you. And this day I will give the carcasses of the camp of the Philistines to the birds of the air and the wild beasts of the earth, that all the earth may know that there is a God in Israel. Then all this assembly shall know that the Lord does not save with sword and spear; for the battle is the Lord's, and He will give you into our hands."*
>
> **1 Samuel 17:44-47**

In the heart of the boy David, was a true desire to destroy the opponent of God and His people. Goliath was a giant—a man who not only had great stature, but came with great taunts against the Israelites. But David was determined to silence the giant once and for all and ensure that God got the victory in the lives of His people. By faith, using only a simple sling, He brought down the enemy. What a picture for us! We too can disarm the enemy of our souls, the one who threatens and humiliates God's people. In the name of Jesus, we can silence Satan and every demon that torments those we love. Let us rise up boldly, pulling down every stronghold and destroying every problem that intimidates us in life. *Amen!*

Knowing Who We Are

Satan and his demons have come in like a flood in this age to destroy the communities and nations in the world. The kingdom of the darkness tries to stir up the peace inside our homes, causing dissent—but sometimes we, the people of God—become willing participants because we give in to the spirit of fear. There is a lesson for us in the account of David and Goliath. Let's see what David focused on when he came face-to-face with his adversary.

The Bible speaks of Goliath as a seasoned warrior whose height was six cubits and a span—about nine feet and three inches tall. I am six feet tall, and just imagining how Goliath must have towered over David is a very frightening thought! As if his height were not intimidating enough, Goliath had been a soldier on the battlefield all his life. 1 Samuel 17 tells us that the armor Goliath wore into battle was incredibly heavy. The head of his spear alone weighed more than sixteen pounds! He came to threaten God's people wearing a bronze helmet of protection on his head, and Goliath was known as 'Champion.'

David, on the other hand, was an ordinary shepherd boy, unfamiliar with the weaponry or armor of soldiers, and from the moment King Saul saw David, he compared the size of the two who were about to face off. There was no way this 'mere youth' could survive! Even the king pictured David as a good-for-nothing shepherd boy who would never be able to kill Goliath.

David, too, never went out thinking he would kill a giant. The story tells that he was simply going to take food to his brothers at the battlefield. He was just a young man, one that even his siblings took no notice of—he was a gentle soul, a boy who loved to play his harp while caring for his father's sheep. The shepherd's job was seen as undesirable and lowly. In contrast, being appointed to become a soldier in the army and fighting on the battlefield was regarded as a high duty and calling. Every family honored a soldier; he would be respected as a warrior of the nation. But David had no such honor.

Running happily towards his brothers, David heard a loud, terrifying voice taunting the armies of Israel and blaspheming Israel's God. The Bible says that this went on for forty days and nights—Goliath repeatedly stood on the top of the mountain and called out to Saul and the armies of Israel to send someone out to fight him. Goliath challenged Saul that if any of his soldiers could kill him, the Philistines would become their servants, but, if they failed to do so, then Israel would be treated as their servants. When Goliath came out and shouted with his thundering voice, the Israelite armies ran in fear and hid themselves. Even Saul, the captain of the army, a man well-trained as a soldier, was afraid of this notorious giant.

He had no idea that the day David entered the army field was also to become the last day of Goliath's breath on earth. I love what the boy says to King Saul when he heard what the giant was saying to the children of God: "Who is this uncircumcised human, that he should defy the armies of the living God?" (1 Samuel 17:26).

This is where David's victory lay! David didn't cower. He didn't see himself as a mere shepherd. *He knew who he was in the eyes of God.* Do you know how encouraging and powerful David's declaration is to me as a pastor and a believer in Jesus?! David didn't worry about anything else; his eyes were fixed directly upon the power and might of the God of Israel. He saw himself and the situation he was in with the eyes of the Spirit. And with that confidence, he boldly offered to fight the giant, to slay this beast of a man and finish him off. *Glory to God Almighty!*

The Israelite armies trembled with fear; they had no faith in the living God. Although they worshipped Him, witnessed His miracles, and served God with every part of their lives, not one of them displayed wholehearted trust in God when challenges hit them. For forty days and nights, they were scared, living in fear, without the courage to approach their enemy. Even King Saul, who was the commander of the armies of Israel, was unable to lead them because he was so intimidated and paralyzed by fear. Yet, this mere boy, with an undesirable body, fit for no army, walked into the midst of the enemy's territory and, without a seed of doubt in his heart, destroyed the giant. *Hallelujah!*

Overcoming the Spirit of Fear

The soldiers of Israel saw Goliath as a giant before them, yet the real giant that loomed large in their minds was the spirit of fear. Fear caused the army to hide, refusing to face their adversary. Fear kept them in a state of panic and uncertainty, immobilized and anxious.

And still today, the spirit of fear grips our world. As Christians, we must recognize that fear is the enemy of our faith. We must not be controlled by a spirit of fear! When fear enters our inner-person, it brings confusion and leaves us emotionally drained and discouraged. Fear is the voice that says you cannot do anything. Through the spirit of fear, the devil speaks intimidation. He traps us with the thought that the threat is too great and that we are nothing. We must know, like David, that we are the children of God, and that He who is in us is greater than he who is in the world (1 John 4:4).

Let's silence the voice of fear once and for all! As long as Satan knows that you are weak and weary, he will continue to manipulate you until you cannot move forward anymore. Let's rise up in faith and destroy the works of the devil so that God can get the victory in our lives, families, churches, and communities. The Bible teaches us that fear and faith can never work together. The two are opposites. This is why feeding on the Word of God is vital; it increases, strengthens and enables our faith in Jesus to grow. Romans 10:17 says that "faith comes by hearing." Hearing what? It is through hearing the voice of Jesus alone. *Amen!*

LIMITLESS FAITH

David was able to challenge Goliath because he had limitless faith in God, the God of Israel that he worshipped and adored. With full confidence in God, he said to Goliath:

> *You come to me with a sword, with a spear, and with a javelin. But I come to you in the name of the Lord of hosts, the God of the armies of Israel, whom you have defied. This day the Lord will deliver you into my hand, and I will strike you and take your head from you. And this day I will give the carcasses of the camp of the Philistines to the birds of the air and the wild beasts of the earth, that all the earth may know that there is a God in Israel. Then all this assembly shall know that the Lord does not save with sword and spear; for the battle is the Lord's, and He will give you into our hands.*
>
> *1 Samuel 17:45-47*

Hallelujah! What a bold heart!

Don't ever allow yourself to be intimidated by the voice of fear in you. When you hear the voice of Satan and fear becomes louder, trying to threaten you, don't just sit there doing nothing. Rise up in the Spirit and use the authority that Jesus gave you. You must prove the devil wrong. Tell him he is a liar and deceiver! In Luke 10:19, Jesus clearly says that we have full authority to trample on all that threatens to harm or hurt us. When you understand the value of God's Word of truth and His mighty power and authority in you, it will be a piece of cake for you to overcome challenges and trials. *Praise Jesus!*

Look at what David did! With his eyes fixed on God and His glory, David won the battle, and in so doing, he proved his brothers, King Saul, and the entire Israelite army, wrong. They had looked down at this mere boy, thinking that he could never be able to slay the giant or destroy him.

Take heart! Others may not see the anointing that is within us, but when we know who we are in Christ, we can lift our head and take on every obstacle in the name of Jesus. When others doubted him, what did David do? He stepped forward, picked the weapons that suited him, and released them with the power of the name of God. How amazing is that?

My friends, when others think you are wrong, snap out of it, ignore the critical and negative words about you, get up, and courageously respond to your problems just as David did. Run with boldness and faith in Jesus. By faith, bring down and destroy all the power and the works of the enemy upon your life, wielding the true Word of God. *Praise the Lord!*

Take a moment to look at your life. *Are any 'Goliaths' threatening you in this season? Are you facing terrifying challenges and trials? Are you going through any struggles in life? Have adversities nearly knocked you back from trusting God?* David saw Goliath as an opportunity to demonstrate the power of his living God. He saw Goliath as nothing, for he knew from his past experiences that his God was greater and stronger than any problem.

Do we look at our problems and challenges as larger than Jesus? As a believer, how do you respond to your own giants, the issues that you are facing right now? When sickness enters your body, do you cry out loud with fear, saying, "I don't want to live, I have enough of this life"? I certainly hope not!

How is your walk with God in this season? Are you finding it difficult to activate the Word of God in the current battle you face? How is your family today? What about your relationship as a husband and wife? What about the financial situation in your family? Are there addictions and desires of the flesh that are intent on destroying the temple of the Spirit of God who dwells in you?

Friends, the list can go on. You and I each have our own giant that needs to be destroyed. And they can seem too great for us. But when we fix our eyes on Jesus, the cares of this world lose their power. When we see through the eyes of the Spirit, the threats of the enemy fade into insignificance.

Right Perspective

The reason the Israelite armies hid away was because they perceived the giant to be larger than the God they served. When they failed to recognize that they were the beloved people of God, they were easily intimidated. This is the enemy's scheme. He sends 'giants' of discouragement and fear to weaken our trust in God and His promises. We must recognize that when we view these 'Goliaths' through human eyes, we are left paralyzed and disabled from our full potential to receive the blessings of God. Whether we face job losses or broken marriages, sickness, homelessness, poverty, loneliness, anxiety, depression, insufficient finances, or even unforgiveness, adultery, or the results of a sinful life, we can be sure that God will win the victory. There is no defeat for God's people when we take our full authority in Christ, assured of who we are in Him, and come fearlessly in His name against every issue we face.

Let us remember that God has already planned and purposed blessings for each of our families. Indeed, some of the biggest 'Goliaths' that are hovering over families today are struggles with finances and broken relationships. How do we come against these giants? God tells us clearly in Malachi 3:10 that we are to bring our tithe into His house. What faith is required to do that even when the voice of the giant within us keeps on pressuring our minds and taunting us with worries! Faith takes God at His Word, while fear says, "What about food for my kids? What about the bills that needs to be paid? What about all the requirements we need to take care of?"

It is these 'little worries' and issues of life that can seem so big. It is the same with our relationships—when they threaten to break down, they can overwhelm us and bring distress and pressure to our spouses and children, and even to the church. There are so many families with relationship difficulties that seem too large to overcome or solve. The spirit of unforgiveness is distressing, and will never take you to your divine destination. Let's heed the warning in Matthew 6:14 and be quick to forgive others. Let us not limit God's power, protection, and provision in our families, but get rid of all anxiety and worry and, rather than focusing on survival, look to Him for abundant breakthrough for all our needs. The Scriptures exhorts us to cast *all our cares* upon Him, because He cares for us (1 Peter 5:7).

When God says that He cares for all our needs, it includes *every* area of our lives: emotional, physical, intellectual, and spiritual. God knows what we lack and promises that He will supply all we need according to His riches in glory (Philippians 4:19). Trust Him with all your heart, and win the battle as you cast all your cares upon Jesus!

WE ARE OVERCOMERS

The Bible talks about the sons and daughters of God as overcomers. We are more than conquerors in Christ Jesus! Romans 8:37-38 says,

> *Yet in all these things we are more than conquerors through Him who loved us. For I am persuaded that*

> *neither death nor life, nor angels nor principalities nor powers, nor things present nor things to come, nor height nor depth, nor any other created thing, shall be able to separate us from the love of God which is in Christ Jesus our Lord.*

Jesus has already won the victory for us, and we are the inheritors of His Kingdom. The battle that we're fighting is spiritual. Ultimately, we wrestle against Satan and his evil forces. That is why Scripture says,

> *. . . your adversary the devil walks about like a roaring lion, seeking whom he may devour. Resist him, steadfast in the faith, knowing that the same sufferings are experienced by your brotherhood in the world. But may the God of all grace, who called us to His eternal glory by Christ Jesus, after you have suffered a while, perfect, establish, strengthen, and settle you. To Him be the glory and the dominion forever and ever. Amen.*
>
> 1 Peter 5:8-11

ARMED FOR VICTORY

In some cases, however, issues and problems happen in our lives simply due to our lack of knowledge and wisdom. One of the realities for the Israelites as they faced Goliath was that none of them knew how to approach the fight. They were used to fighting armies of regular soldiers—now they were faced with a solitary giant who terrified them with his words. How were the Israelites to meet this threat?

Should they march onto the battlefield as usual? They needed to know *how* to fight this unusual battle!

Often, we too fail to find victory because we lack of knowledge and wisdom on how to proceed in face of the enemy. This is why we must turn to the Word of God. The Word is our sword and faith is our shield. With the armor of God firmly in place, we can never be defeated! When we put on the armor of God, we will live in victory, knowing we are covered and protected from head to toe. *Amen!*

Our spiritual armor is more effective than any physical protection we may acquire. Do you know what happened to Saul and his armies? They wore their battle-armor from head to toe, but they had no faith in God, or even in their own abilities. As the people of God, we must not rely on our own understanding or on human ways of coping. We must wear the full armor of God.

The *helmet of salvation* is vital, for it protects your ears from what you hear, your mind from what you think, and your eyes from what you see. The *belt of truth* protects us from the cunning lies of Satan and from his evil intent. The *breastplate of righteousness* assures us that we are perfect in Christ—that we are forgiven and worthy to bear His name. We wear *shoes* upon our feet that represent the readiness of the Gospel of peace—they ensure that wherever we go, we turn chaos to calm, and that the Prince of Peace fights our battles with us. The Word of God is the *sword of the spirit*, the weapon that speaks against the enemy and makes Satan tremble and flee. And we raise up our *shield of faith*, declaring that God is greater than all our foes! *Hallelujah!*

As we clothe ourselves in spiritual armor, let us remember that Jesus paid the cost of our redemption for us on the cross. He took all our fears, insecurities, sicknesses, infirmities, poverty, and so forth. There is no blessing and no deliverance He has not won for us! Let us remind the devil of Jesus' victory for us on the cross, activating the Word of God as we engage with the enemy. Let us break the habit of using our own physical mindsets and words to solve issues that can be easily overcome through the work of the Spirit and the Word of Jesus. *Amen!*

> *But be doers of the word, and not hearers only, deceiving yourselves. For if anyone is a hearer of the word and not a doer, he is like a man observing his natural face in a mirror; for he observes himself, goes away, and immediately forgets what kind of man he was.*
>
> **James 1:22-25**

Yes, be a doer of the Word. Be one that loves to activate and perform the living Word of God. There are so many Christians who question why trouble keeps happening in their families. Is this because we only hear the Word, but do not do it? We must teach the Word of God in our homes, putting it into practice and bringing forgiveness to one another. We must not allow bitterness to creep in, or give the devil a foothold. When the living Word of truth is loved and valued in our homes, we will know how to overcome when troubles and problems hit us. As we activate the Word of God, we will see that our problems are simply giants that can be overthrown!

BOLDLY DECLARE YOUR VICTORY

As David stepped forward to fight his enemy, he walked straight towards Goliath and faced him boldly. We must do the same when we bring out the Word of God to defeat the problems that arise against us. For example, when the doctor says that you only have a few months to live, you need to rise up and use the Word of God to speak life and health to your body.

Say, "I am the son (or daughter) of the Living God, and I do not accept the spirit of death! I declare that God will give me more days to live, and that I will enjoy my loved ones and His blessings in my life. I declare and decree to my body in the mighty name of Jesus, that by the stripes and the blood of Jesus, I am completely healed!"

It only takes a seed of faith to move mountains! When you're facing problems, rise up as an alert warrior. Retrieve the Word of God from within you, and speak against your situation.

> *So Jesus said to them, ". . . if you have faith as a mustard seed, you will say to this mountain, 'Move from here to there,' and it will move; and nothing will be impossible for you. However, this kind does not go out except by prayer and fasting."*
>
> **Matthew 17:20-21**

A great shift takes place when we do things in life, not by might, nor by strength, but by the Spirit of God (Zechariah 4:6). Let's take a look again at what David did to Goliath.

Amazingly, the moment David released that first stone, it hit Goliath's head right between the eyes, and then *bang*, he collapsed! It is the same for us, the children of God. The minute we release the living Word of Jesus with faith, every attack on our lives will be immediately void. David targeted the head of the giant and by hitting him right between the eyes, he brought the whole body down.

Likewise, we must target the spiritual root of the problems we face. The Spirit of God helps us know where to aim, and the Word of God is the 'stone' that you can release by faith against your problems. His Word is powerful against the sicknesses and health problems in your life. It can fix the broken relationship issues within your home. It can get straight to the root of financial problems in your families.

Once we release His Word, we will see these strongholds and giants fall, destroyed in the mighty name of Jesus. In other words, your spiritual weapons only work when you are led by the Spirit of God, and believe and activate the Word of God by *faith*!

OBEDIENT TO HIS SPIRIT

What about the idea of obedience?

> *Samuel said: "Has the Lord as great delight in burnt offerings and sacrifices, as in obeying the voice of the Lord? Behold, to obey is better than sacrifice, and to heed than the fat of rams."*
>
> **1 Samuel 15:22**

God loves those who walks in obedience to His words and principles. Are you obeying God's Word of truth or are you living like a rebellious or lukewarm Christian in this season? God's heart is for us to be doers of His Word. His promises and blessings are eternal and everlasting. If we walk by faith and not by sight, living in obedience and not just commitment, then every time we proclaim His Word, God's angels will move forth to fight for us and fulfil our needs. *Thank You, Father God!*

It was through the obedience of Abraham that he laid hold of blessings for his household and a home for God's people in the promised land. It was the obedience of Noah that saved his family from the flood and brought new life to the world. Through the obedience of Moses, the Israelites came out of Egypt even though he felt inadequate to speak to Pharaoh. Because David ran after the heart of God and obeyed His laws and commandments, God made a covenant with him that his royal lineage would continue through generations. And then there is the greatest display of obedience that we could ever learn from—our Lord Jesus, who, though it cost Him His life, obeyed the will of God the Father, because He loves us so much. *Hallelujah!*

Beloved of Jesus, as successors of Christ and inheritors of His Kingdom, it is our obligation to follow His footsteps, obey His Word, and serve Him according to what He commands. If we continue to abide in Jesus, we will become stronger and braver in the face of the enemy, and in the strength and authority of the Lord, we will dismantle every problem that threatens to destroy our love, peace and joy.

Prayer and Fasting

Some enemies require determination from us in order to conquer them. When the disciples failed to see a demon defeated, Jesus told them, "This kind does not go out except by prayer and fasting" (Matthew 17:21). God moves when we seek Him diligently and wholeheartedly through prayer and fasting. Through faithful intercession, we come before His throne of grace. The more we seek Him and His presence, the clearer we will hear His voice and be able to clarify how He wants us to respond against any trials or threat. *Thank You, Lord!*

In Acts 13, David is described as, "a man after God's own heart." This should be the same for you and me—God has set His love on us; now we must run after God's heart and share His desires. David won the battle against Goliath because he had faith in his loving, living God. Prayer and fasting are ways we deny ourselves and allow the Spirit to take the lead in our lives. David won the battle, not because he relied on his physical strength and abilities, but because he went forth in the power of the Holy Spirit, believing in his living God, and the power of His Word. Through prayer and fasting, great men and women in the Bible overcame their giants!

Prayer and fasting draws you closer to God, and conveys a posture of humility as you seek His heart. These spiritual weapons enable us to hear His voice with clarity. Through prayer and fasting, Esther and Daniel overcame the greatest trials and danger of their lives. In the same way, all the great prophets and disciples in the Bible showed their obedience and repentance—with a contrite spirit, they drew near to the heart of God, asking for help in times of desperate need.

God will often bless specific requests, pouring out His grace upon us, when we not only obey and activate the Word of God by faith, but when we seek Him with all our heart through prayer and fasting. I tell you the truth, you will witness the favor and blessings of God upon your family, churches, and nation. You will see your children blessed. Your workplace will be blessed. Financial circumstances will become blessed, and God's favor and goodness will follow you and your family. You will marvel and be amazed by how God blesses you when you seek Him through prayer and fasting. *Hallelujah!*

TRUST IN YOURSELF

David didn't use his muscles or strength to fight against Goliath—he fought and won by trusting God wholeheartedly. But he also trusted his own instincts. This is a key to our breakthrough too. David had already seen the strength God had given him when he killed the lion and the bear at his father's sheep-farm. He trusted in God—but he was also a willing vessel. David was determined to use the battle as an opportunity to bring glory to the name of the Lord and deliver His people from danger. He assessed the situation with confidence through eyes of faith, maintaining his boldness and keeping focused upon the power of his living God, as well as trusting his own instincts and abilities. With that powerful combination in play, David knew that the victory was already his!

Enabled by His Spirit, we can experience the satisfaction of knowing that we have partnered with the Lord for the outcome we desired and prayed for. When we believe in Him, God goes ahead of us, preparing the way for us to take ground for Him and His people. He gives us the victory! It's that simple! Philippians 4:13 says that we can do all things through Christ Jesus who strengthens us. When we trust God with all our heart, mind and soul, everything around us works as we believed and expected!

Do not listen when people criticize you or say you cannot do something that God has placed in your heart. Reject the words that you are nothing, that you are useless, or that you can never be successful. You need to do as David did—trust your conscience and your abilities, but most importantly, put your full trust in God's Word and promises. Always remember that Jesus is your victory. The battle belongs to God. But remember that God loves to work through His people. We are equipped in every way to do His will. Let's allow the Lord to examine our hearts to see whether we fervently believe Him or not, when He reminds us of the gift and call on our lives.

STAY FAITH-FILLED

Some people have become weary in the fight of faith. They have fought a long time and have become discouraged. The

Bible says that Jesus is our strength in times of suffering and pain. He comforts and embraces us with His peace, love and grace. No weapon formed against you shall prosper (Isaiah 54:17). Just remember, God requires our own positive and faith-filled response before He will fight on our behalf. Sometimes, we don't even need to fight the battle. When we trust Him deeply, God says the battles belongs to Him and He will fight for us. So even if you are hurting or feel defeated, trust in Him will all your heart. He can turn what the devil meant for evil into an opportunity for your blessing!

TRAIN THE NEXT GENERATION

We must train and equip our children so they can destroy their own giants. We serve and worship a great and mighty God who is bigger than our problems. I want to encourage mothers and fathers to train and equip your children in the Word and ways of God. Develop and teach them in the Spirit so they can overcome any challenges and trials in life. I promise you that when they grow up, they will never depart from it. It will be a threat to Satan and the kingdom of darkness if your children are well prepared and equipped in the Word of Jesus and the power of His Spirit. *Praise God!*

> *Behold, children are a heritage from the Lord, the fruit of the womb is a reward. Like arrows in the hand of a warrior, so are the children of one's youth.*
>
> **Psalm 127:3-4**

Let us shepherd and lead our young ones with diligence. It is sad to witness so many incidents on the streets involving the lives of the young generation. So many precious children's lives have been destroyed at such a young age. Why is this? The mission of Satan is to steal, kill and destroy. Therefore, before we release our children into the world as sharp arrows for the glory of God, we must fulfil our duty and obligation as parents to guide and train them, ensuring they are familiar with the spiritual weapons they need to destroy their own giants or enemies.

Our children are very special in the master plan of Jesus. They are the soldiers of Christ who will faithfully take His Good News to all the ends of the world, if they are well trained in the Spirit and the law of the Lord.

We have looked at the story of David. He was a mere shepherd-boy who had been trained well by the Spirit of God, not only by taking care of the sheep, but by meditating in the presence of the Lord while playing his harp. He became a warrior for God's people and His Glory even at a young age. David had been brought up in a family surrounded by the laws and commandments of God. It was no coincidence, then, that serving the needs of others and worshipping the living God was David's passion. This was what his tender yet bold and faithful heart yearned for. He learned to trust God and depend on Him through the battles and trials that he faced. He cared deeply for the wellbeing of his flock. The Bible says that, when an animal came to attack the sheep, David rose and snatched the sheep from the mouth of its aggressor. May our children do likewise! When Satan comes to snatch away their blessings, may they rise in the Spirit to defend themselves and destroy their giants in the power of Jesus!

If our children are to triumph over the lies and schemes of the enemy and survive on the battlefield of this world, we must:

- Teach them the Word of God
- Train them in the ways of the Spirit
- Equip them to put on the full amour of God; and
- Set apart consistent time to spiritually support them during suffering and trials.

I assure you, Jesus and His Holy Word is the answer to every problem our children face. We cannot resolve their problems any other way. We must equip them to fight their battles. You will not live with anxiety or stress as a parent when you know that your child is well-prepared to face the giants in their own lives.

When David went to fight Goliath, *he already knew* that God would stand and fight for him. David *already knew* that Goliath was no problem to him. In fact, the only real problem he saw was the Israelites armies quivering with fear and anxiety. This is the same problem that influences us today. It is not hard for God to save us if we walk in obedience and abide in His Word of truth. As sons and daughters of the Living God, we must know who we are in Jesus Christ! Whatever sickness we may be going through or problem we are seeking to eradicate—whether at home, in our workplaces, or even in our own personal lives—be reminded that nothing is impossible to God. *Hallelujah!*

Keep your eyes focused upon Jesus and the reward of eternal life. Remember to bring down and destroy the 'giant within'—don't ever allow the problems you face to weaken your spirit or discourage your faith in God. Don't let these challenges compromise you or cause you to hide in fear and insecurity. If David knew that the God that he served was greater than the trials he faced, then we must believe and do the same. If David can bring down and destroy his Goliath the giant, so can you! *Amen!*

Family of Christ, these end days are not easy at all. Satan is seeking to remove you from God's place of safety and keep you from the blessing that comes from being in His divine will. He is intent on destroying your families. He wants to fill your mind with garbage. But we are not unaware of his schemes! Press on. Be on guard and be prepared to rise up like a warrior in God's Kingdom. Remind yourself of your identity as a believer in Christ. You must move in power and learn to stand in your full authority, with the armor of God upon you and the sword of the Spirit which is the word of truth abiding deep within in you. Together, let us be those who put the enemy under our feet so that we may take hold of life and blessing for ourselves and the generations to come.

Dear God, today we long to keep up in the Spirit and learn to move by faith. We desire to live a life of obedience to You and be doers of Your Word. Draw near to us as we meditate on Your Word and seek You. We stand in the power and authority of the name and take the blood of Jesus to fight against the enemy. Today we declare that the battle belongs to You, God. Our great and mighty God is fighting for us! Our warfare with the enemy is spiritual, and so we arm ourselves in the Spirit. Your Word says that faith pleases Your heart. We desire to serve You, and to bring down the 'Goliaths' in our lives. Today, we choose to walk by faith, and not by sight. Praise and honor to You forever and ever, Lord Jesus. Amen!

PRAYER OF SALVATION

If you would like to experience and receive what Jesus made available for you through His resurrection power, and make Him Lord and Savior in your life, I urge you to pray this special prayer with me:

> *Dear God, I desperately need you right now. I admit with a humble heart that I am a sinner. I am sorry for the way that I have lived my life, and I ask for your forgiveness. I confess with my mouth and believe in my heart that Jesus Christ is Lord. I declare that He died on the cross for my sins and rose again on the third day. In this moment, I ask you, Jesus, to enter my heart. Be the personal Lord and Savior of my life. I invite Your Holy Spirit to guide and transform me into a new creation who brings honor and glory to Your name. Thank You, Jesus, for forgiving my sins. According to Your infallible Word of life, I am now saved. In Your mighty name, Jesus, I pray. Amen!*

As you step into your new life in Christ, reach out to a church near you, or tell us of your decision so that we may come alongside you! The following Scriptures will also help you as you become established in your faith:

John 3:16, Romans 10:9-10, Ephesians 2:8-9, 1 John 1:9, Acts 16:31, Psalm 62:1, Acts 2:21, Luke 19:10, 2 Timothy 1.

To God be the Glory Forever and Ever, Amen!

AUTHOR'S NOTE

Throughout this book I have shared Scripture, along with some of my own personal experiences—the good, the struggles, and the victories—but what I most long for you to hear is the Gospel of Jesus Christ. Throughout my spiritual journey (of more than twenty years), I have come across so many people who live in defeat and fear, listening to the lies of Satan.

I, too, have fought my own giants, and became weary and discouraged at times. Despite that, I praise God for His Word of truth. I have received the abundance of Jesus upon my life, as well as the lives of my families and friends. I have learnt so much along the way as God has kindly disciplined, corrected, equipped and trained me, preparing me for His good works. Without the power of the Holy Spirit, and the Word of truth, I truly would not have been able to overcome the giants I needed to in order to share these words of encouragement to strengthen and empower you as well.

Wherever you may be on your personal Christian journey right now, one thing I know for sure: The Word of God is life to our bodies, minds and souls. Only the Word of Jesus can set you free and bring victory to your circumstances. Nothing is impossible with God, if you truly believe in Him! Just remember, as a son and daughter of God, you are *more than a conqueror* through Christ Jesus our Lord. It is all about Jesus and His salvation; and the power of His Holy Spirit upon your life. Continue to trust Him and His Word of promise!

I pray that this book has brought fresh 'manna' to your soul, that through its pages you have been encouraged and strengthened and that fresh hope has been ministered into your life. All that I have shared in this book has come from years of ministry within my family, friends and especially my local church and community.

With a humble heart, I thank you for allowing me to share the Word of God with you. Keep on meditating on God's Word and His laws. Through His commandments, He makes you wiser than your enemies (Psalm 119:97-98). His Word alone is the lamp to our feet and light to our path (Psalm 119:105).

Last but not least, may you enjoy the 'victory of Jesus.' I release blessings upon you, your family, and friends. I speak life into your relationships, your finances, your education, and your circumstances. I speak healing upon your body, mind and soul in Jesus' mighty name. *Amen!*

I want to leave you with this powerful prayer of blessing.

Beloved,

> *The Lord bless you and keep you; The Lord make His face shine upon you, and be gracious to you; The Lord lift up His countenance upon you, and give you peace.*
>
> **Numbers 6:24-26**

I love you, in Jesus' Name!

ACKNOWLEDGEMENTS

To our Worship Centre Christian Church Worldwide, my local church at Divine Revelation Worship Centre, and my family and friends in Christ:

Your unfailing love, encouragement, constant prayer and support for me and my family, especially in regard to the role entrusted to us in God's Kingdom, has benefited us beyond measure. The environment of biblical teaching and spiritual training that you have all cultivated over many years has provided me with a firm foundation, and it is my joy to join you in that endeavor. Your good deeds and kindness have not gone unnoticed, and are recorded in heavenly books of remembrance. You are a means of divine blessing in my life, and I praise God for all of you! Glory to God!

With a thankful heart, I want to acknowledge all my spiritual mentors and teachers of the Word who have shaped my journey as a believer of Christ from 1998, all the way through to the present:

Apostle Viliamu Mafo'e & First Lady, Lavina Mafo'e

Founders & Chairman, Worship Centre Christian Church Worldwide
Senior Pastors, Samoa Worship Centre Christian Church—Apia, Samoa

The Late Ma'anaima Aloalii & First Lady, Olive F Aloalii

Senior Pastors, Samoa Mangere Worship Centre Christian Church—Auckland, New Zealand (2000-2004)

Pastor Leuli Ieriko & First Lady, Eloi Ieriko

Senior Pastors, Samoa Mangere Worship Centre Christian Church—Auckland, New Zealand
Assistant Secretary, Worship Centre Christian Church Worldwide

Pastor To'outa Aloalii & First Lady, Palolo Aloalii

Senior Pastors, His Grace Worship Centre Christian Church—Victoria, Australia
Vice Chairman, Worship Centre Christian Church Worldwide

Second to the Holy Spirit, you have been incredible influences as spiritual and biblical mentors of the Word of God throughout my faith journey. I praise and exalt Jesus for all of you! From the bottom of my heart, thank you all so much. May God bless you all abundantly! *Glory to Jesus!*

ABOUT THE AUTHOR

Melagitone Simanu was born and raised in Samoa by his beloved parents, the late Faleao Ieru and Situpu Sapolu, with a firm Christian faith that believes in the Trinity; God the Father, God the Son and God the Holy Spirit. He has been a born-again Christian since his early twenties. After migrating from Samoa to New Zealand in 2000, he served with the Samoa Mangere Worship Centre Christian Church in Auckland as church Elder and Overseer of the Worship Team Ministry, and later as an Associate Pastor. Since that time he has also served faithfully behind the scenes, setting up band equipment and working on sound desks to facilitate the church in worship.

In 2015, Melagitone and his family moved to Melbourne, where he continued to serve as an Associate Pastor of Shekinah Glory Worship Centre Christian Church in Craigieburn until in 2018 he was appointed and called to serve as Senior Pastor of his local church, the Divine Revelation Worship Centre Christian Church, in Melton, Victoria.

Melagitone Simanu loves to build and lead his family with the Word of God and to fellowship in His presence during worship. He has been happily married since 1998, and is a faithful and devoted husband to his wife, Mareta, and father to daughters Shalom and Lynette, who are a constant source of love, prayers and support for his calling. Pastor Melagitone is well respected and adored by his family, friends and the body of Christ in his community. His passion is to honor the Word of God and open doors of opportunity for his family to activate their gift of music and song writing. Together, they formed the *Divine Kingdom Praises,* ministry team and in 2020, released their first Gospel album, 'Yours Forevermore,' which now ministers to listeners worldwide.

YOURS FOREVERMORE

NOW AVAILABLE FOR PURCHASE OR DOWNLOAD!

Written and Recorded live by the Divine Kingdom Praises family, this collection of anointed worship songs was first released in 2020 to revive the souls of the weary, break chains of fear and oppression, and minister the Gospel of Jesus to those who are lost.

8 ORIGINAL SONGS

Ia Viia Oe
Yours Forevermore
Jesus Loves Me
E Lelei Oe Le Ali'i
My Soul Praise the Lord
Show Me Your Ways
You Are My Peace
Mighty and Faithful God

CD ORDERS

Contact Divine Kingdom Praises on Facebook, or email divinepm7@gmail.com

STREAMING

via Apple Music, iTunes, Spotify, YouTube, TikTok and more.